D1528284

Three Gifted Women
Our Story

Joann, Cindy & Aleja

Three Gifted Women

ISBN: 9798575668299

[signatures]

DEDICATION

We would like to dedicate this book to our many
wonderful Spirit Guides and loved ones who have crossed
over.

Also, a big thank you to our family and friends who
continue to support us on this journey.

CONTENTS

ACKNOWLEDGEMENTS

Many thanks to our wonderful clients for making us who
we are today.

Many thanks to Aleja Estronza, our Reiki Practitioner
who wears many hats, for our great graphics and
photography along with our wonderful website.

A special thanks to
Steve Gingo, our dear friend and Paranormal Investigator
&
Dorann Weber, our friend and very talented photographer
who supplied the beautiful photos for this book.

INTRODUCTION

Every time the three of us go on an adventure, it never seems to happen without some chaos. Whether we are being chased by a group of spiritual beings, reliving the emotions and details of a devastating fire that occurred long ago, hearing the brutal testimonies of former Revolutionary war soldiers or slaves, or experiencing something that we simply cannot explain, not one of our outings has ever been boring. One of our clients' favorite pastimes is to listen to us recount our crazy stories, and every time we do this, they exclaim, "You guys just have to write a book!" Here at long last is our book, which has been both a growth experience and a labor of love, full of passion from beginning to end, telling our stories of how it all began.

This book is divided into three parts. Part I explores the lives and spiritual development of Joann, Cindy, and Aleja. It is an autobiographical account of our childhoods, the unique abilities and sensitivities we each experienced from a young age, and how we nurtured these talents as we grew into adulthood. It is an intimate glimpse into our early lives and how our unique paths led each of us to answer the call to use our gifts to help others.

Part II highlights the stories and adventures of the three of us on the road. We learned a new respect for Spirit after experiencing drained equipment batteries and some frightening episodes being chased in Williamsburg,

Virginia. We spent a wonderful evening discovering many interesting stories while conducting a paranormal investigation of a beautiful old home in Pennington, New Jersey where our audience of skeptics became believers. We also stumbled upon an old hotel that was a former brothel where a suspected murder occurred. Throughout these journeys working together, we learned more and more about the spiritual connection between the three of us.

Part III highlights Joann, Cindy, and Aleja's work through the voices of our clients, and the book concludes with some of the most important lessons we have learned together throughout this journey. As we all turn pages, creating new chapters in our lives, we know and accept that there are always changes ahead. These changes have allowed us to continually expand who we are while working on the "Healing of the Mind, Body & Soul" of others.

"Psychics in Development"

PART I:
THREE GIFTED WOMEN

JOANN

"I truly believe that if your head is not where your heart is, then you will never feel complete. Your heart is ALWAYS in the driver's seat." ~Joann

As my journey through life started, I can remember that I always felt different. I felt like an adult and always wanted to fix something or someone. I was empathic, sensitive, forever wanting to help -- a real people pleaser. I never wanted to disappoint anyone. I would always make sure, or at least try to, that the people around me were happy and that others' needs came first. I am still very much the same way.

I have always believed that these traits were ingrained in me, and I later learned that they were part of my genetics. My paternal great-grandmother had moved to this country from Italy, and she had her very own special spiritual gifts. My father told me that when I was an infant, she was put into a psychiatric hospital named Greystone. This was in her later years when she was diagnosed with what they thought was Alzheimer's. In that day and age people did not fully understand psychic ability. We often wondered if her psychic ability was misdiagnosed as Alzheimer's or another mental condition.

At the time of my birth, my great-grandmother was in her final days at Greystone. One day she demanded that my father bring me there so that she could meet her great-granddaughter. My father agreed and brought me to the hospital. He placed me in her arms. She then touched my hand and my arm gently and she spoke to me in Italian. She said, "Questo è un bellissimo angelo!" which means "What a beautiful angel!" She turned to my grandfather, her son, and said, "Questo bambino aiuterà gli altri," which means, "This child will help others!" I do believe that I was born with my psychic abilities as part of my soul and my DNA and that my soul already knew that this was who I was to become in this lifetime. But I also believe that my great-grandmother, who had these abilities as well, through her touch transferred her energy to me to help assist and define who I was to become.

One of her special gifts was healing. She had the ability to remove "Maloik" from people, better known as the evil eye to non-Italians. This evil eye is a malevolent look that is believed to cause ill or harm on someone when it is directed at them. It is believed in many cultures to affect people in the form of misfortune, disease, or injury. Most often, it is also accompanied by a headache. People in the neighborhood who believed they were cursed with this evil eye would come flocking to my great-grandmother. She would sit them down in a chair, hold a dish of water over their head and pray over them. By tradition, the prayer to remove the evil eye must be recited in Italian. She would then use her pinky to drop oil into the dish. It was believed that how many circles there were and how far the oil spread in the dish was directly related to how much jealous energy was aimed at the person. She would repeat this process three times. My father has told me that many people would come from miles around seeking her help. My great-grandmother was a very kind, trustworthy and generous woman. She would deliver messages, using her intuition, to those she felt needed direction, never turning anyone away.

Many people ask whether there is any truth to this curse, the evil eye. I am not sure if we will ever know the answer, but I am sure that my great-grandmother helped many people both spiritually and physically. As far back as I can remember, and even now when I have a bad headache, a family friend who is a very sweet old

4

Italian lady will pray over me much like my great-grandmother did for others. I always feel better within hours, so there must be some truth to this belief.

As a young child, my creative imagination and my empathy towards others began to manifest in different ways. For example, I had a very best friend at the time whose name was Jerry. One might ask who is Jerry? Jerry was my "hubbin," also known as my husband. Yes, that is what I called him. He was a dummy doll that a ventriloquist would use. My mom had a husband, and my grandmother, and my aunts, so why not me too? My mom always told me, and I also vividly remember, that I had the best imagination as a child. I would play for hours by myself. I would line up my dolls and stuffed animals as they were my friends and companions. I would pretend to be a pet store owner, a waitress, a hairdresser, a teacher, or a singer and a dancer for all my dolls and my stuffed animals. Most importantly I wanted to be a Mom.

No matter who I was with or where I was, I would often find myself being entertained by the people around me. I would focus on their interactions with others and their body language, as if I knew what they would be doing next. Most children whose parents would take them to the zoo would be fascinated by the animals. Not me! While most children were busy feeding the animals, I was more focused on all the people walking around the zoo, and I could strike up a conversation with just about anyone.

Another early indicator of my abilities was my frequent experience of déjà vu. I would be somewhere and suddenly I would get a strong impression that I had been there before. Whether it was a certain situation I was in, or people that I had never met, everything seemed familiar to me. I would often feel that I had experienced this all before. Was it from a past life, I would wonder? I always felt that I was an old soul. I was drawn to certain time periods and places, particularly Colonial Times and the Old West. Perhaps I had been married to a cowboy? Maybe he was not a Prince, but he still rode a horse! These fascinations became more and more prevalent as I grew older. This also held true for people who would come across my path. I would feel very drawn to certain people, while I just wanted to run from others. Once again, was this a case of old souls that I was reconnecting to from past lives?

The most telling sign of things to come was my experience in the dark. I really disliked bedtime. Nighttime in general was not a good time for me. When children are young, they often do not like the dark or to be alone. This was especially true for me because I often saw shadow-like figures or a white mist. I now understand this to mean that I am in the presence of Spirit. I would give my parents such a hard time about going to sleep and never wanted to go into my bedroom alone. It did not help that I slept on the third floor which was situated much like an attic, next to my

6

grandmother's room. At night, it was dark and creepy up there. I would tell my dad, "Daddy, there is a man in the corner of my room." I can still remember that man standing in the corner. My dad's response to me was always, "Stop making things up Joann, and go to sleep." My mom did not believe me either. Here they go again, thinking it's all just my imagination or an excuse to not go to sleep. I was quite the night owl. I can remember that my dad would usually stay with me until I fell asleep, or so he thought. When he left to go to bed himself, I would sneak into my parents' bedroom complaining that I did not feel well and asking if I could sleep with them. As I got older, I usually ended up sleeping in the living room on the couch right next to their room.

You would think that I was simply afraid of the dark like most children, but I was afraid of the man standing in the corner of my room dressed in a black suit with a black Fedora hat on. I could see him quite clearly. He always stood there on guard, clear as day. We eventually moved to a new home and he disappeared for a while. Then one day he returned. This time he stood by the front door. I remember sleeping on the couch that evening when I saw him. I called for my mom, telling her, "Mom, there is a man in a black suit with a black Fedora hat on standing at the front door." She told me no one was there and to go back to sleep. Once again, I was in a situation where I was trying to explain what I was experiencing but was unable to get anyone to comprehend or believe in what I was trying to say. My family, like so many others, were skeptics.

The vision I was seeing in the dark was finally validated one day when my mom and I were looking through old photos. I came across a picture of a man in a black suit with a black Fedora hat in his hand. I was excited and I said to my mom, "This is the guy at the front door. He is the one that comes at night that I have told you about!" She was stunned and she told me that this was a photo of her father who had died years before I was born. I said to my mom, "Well, he must be visiting you and grandma!" This was the first time I had ever received validation about seeing Spirit which made me think, "Is this for real? Can I really see Spirits?"

Spirits love the dark, be it dark rooms, corners, attics or basements. Therefore, they tend to visit their loved ones in the evening. Spirits will often come to me at night when I am not preoccupied with the hustle and bustle of life. Spirits have no concept of time because time does not exist in the next dimension which we call the "other side." But for me, being an open portal to the other side, Spirit does not realize that sleep is important in this dimension when our soul is in a physical body. I have figured out that in this lifetime, between talking to Spirit and dealing with my own daily events, there is simply not going to be much sleep in the equation.

When you are a young girl, sleepover parties are common. A bunch of girls getting together, painting their nails, eating snacks, dancing and acting silly, and of course talking about boys! I attended these parties until it came time to go to sleep. I just couldn't do it. I couldn't sleep at other people's houses! Once the lights went out, the shadows would come in. My poor parents made many trips in the wee hours of the night to pick me up from these parties when I said I didn't feel well. Not feeling well was my typical excuse to leave. Although shadows would still come out at home, I felt safer there.

As I grew from a child to a teenager, so did my ability, but I did not want it to. After all, being a teenager was hard enough without this complication. Throughout my teenage years my empathy for people never changed. I could often sense things about people such as if they were sick, sad, going to have a car accident, potential break up in a relationship, and many other things. I was afraid to tell my family or friends for fear of them not accepting me or thinking I was crazy. If my family did not understand, what would make me think my friends would? I often chose to not talk about it. However, I would sometimes say to my friends, "Boy I have this gut feeling that… "xyz" is happening or is going to happen." Guess what? It almost always did! After a while my friends started paying attention and would joke and say, "Wow, what is Joann's "gut feeling" saying about this?" As I learned years later, this information was flowing to me from my Spirit Guides. This information was very real. I was not crazy. I was just simply different.

I remember being eighteen and having a dream that I was in my yellow Firebird, which was my car at the time. I had stopped at a traffic light and looked to my right. There was a man on a bright blue motorcycle dressed in black leather, with a full-face motorcycle helmet. He flipped his face shield up from his helmet to reveal the most stunning blue eyes I had ever seen. I thought to myself, "Wow! He is so handsome!" All these years later I still remember this "dream." Or so I thought it was a dream. Many years later I met a man who became a very special person in my life. He was identical to the image in my "dream," right down to the blue motorcycle, dressed in black leather with blue eyes. Dream? No! I now know that this was a premonition. This premonition that I received was of an encounter that I would face along my life's journey.

A premonition is somewhat like a dream, except you have a strong emotional attachment to it, and you remember it for days, months, and years later. When you have a dream, there is not an emotional attachment. A dream may cause you to wake up and feel emotions, but they disappear quickly. You will also forget the details of the dream shortly after you wake up.

Another thing I noticed growing up was that I often visualized situations before they occurred. I have always had sharp visualization skills, and almost everything I visualized seemed to happen. My graduation party, the guy I would date after graduation, the car I would buy, the home I later purchased,

remodeled and curr
all seen before they c
myself if this was all a c
power of my mind, knowing w
would get it, and expecting nothing

Later in life, when I came to learn about
world and manifesting, I realized that manifesta
based upon the Law of Attraction. When you put
intention out into the Universe, that's manifestation
Visualization is an aid to help you to manifest what you
want. If you see the end result, this helps to bring your
intention toward you. Our mind is very powerful, and
most of us don't even begin to tap into it. When you put
positivity out into the universe, you will get it back.
Putting negativity out into the universe will attract that
also.

Eventually I became interested in other psychics and
their ability to just seem to know things like I did. I felt
comfortable around them because they understood me
and the things I was experiencing. I can remember
asking my mom to take me to visit a Psychic Reader that
someone recommended to us. To my surprise my mom
was actually open to the idea. After she experienced this
first reading, she became a believer. I have been to
many psychics over the years, some better than others.
Some would tell me things like what I would do after I
graduated high school. Boys were always a popular
subject that would come up during a reading. What
teenage girl didn't want to know if Prince Charming was

, give

myself
nother's
psychic
ways felt
I learned
iem when
s use tarot
ymbols and
ig a regular
nt meanings
, crystal balls
and looking into ⌐ ⌐   sual guidance.
When throwing the runes, which a.⌐   es, interpreting
how they land and what sequence they are in is yet
another tool. A good Psychic Reader must still have
their own intuition and ability to connect to their Guides
and Spirit, no matter what tools they choose to use.

I felt that the world of spirit was not nearly as
frightening as scary movies. These movies were NOT
for me because I found that they were much more
exaggerated than the spirit world. If I watched one, I
would be sleeping with the light on for weeks.
Ironically, years later, I was attracted to the paranormal.
I liked watching paranormal investigation shows on TV
and seeing how all the evidence came together. I now
enjoy collaborating and doing investigations with my
peers who are paranormal investigators. During the

remodeled and currently live in, the dog I wanted, were all seen before they came to be. I would often ask myself if this was all a coincidence or if it was the power of my mind, knowing what I wanted, believing I would get it, and expecting nothing less.

Later in life, when I came to learn about the spiritual world and manifesting, I realized that manifestation was based upon the Law of Attraction. When you put your intention out into the Universe, that's manifestation. Visualization is an aid to help you to manifest what you want. If you see the end result, this helps to bring your intention toward you. Our mind is very powerful, and most of us don't even begin to tap into it. When you put positivity out into the universe, you will get it back. Putting negativity out into the universe will attract that also.

Eventually I became interested in other psychics and their ability to just seem to know things like I did. I felt comfortable around them because they understood me and the things I was experiencing. I can remember asking my mom to take me to visit a Psychic Reader that someone recommended to us. To my surprise my mom was actually open to the idea. After she experienced this first reading, she became a believer. I have been to many psychics over the years, some better than others. Some would tell me things like what I would do after I graduated high school. Boys were always a popular subject that would come up during a reading. What teenage girl didn't want to know if Prince Charming was ever going to show up and when? They would also give me some messages about friends and family.

In my last year of high school, I found myself spending a lot of time at my best friend's grandmother's house. She was very much interested in the psychic world, as she was a Psychic Reader herself. I always felt very comfortable and connected to this world. I learned that psychics use various tools to assist them when doing a psychic read. Some psychic readers use tarot cards or gypsy cards, as these cards show symbols and pictures, which have a meaning. When using a regular deck of cards, each card has many different meanings depending on where it is placed. Tea leaves, crystal balls and looking into a glass of water aid in visual guidance. When throwing the runes, which are stones, interpreting how they land and what sequence they are in is yet another tool. A good Psychic Reader must still have their own intuition and ability to connect to their Guides and Spirit, no matter what tools they choose to use.

I felt that the world of spirit was not nearly as frightening as scary movies. These movies were NOT for me because I found that they were much more exaggerated than the spirit world. If I watched one, I would be sleeping with the light on for weeks. Ironically, years later, I was attracted to the paranormal. I liked watching paranormal investigation shows on TV and seeing how all the evidence came together. I now enjoy collaborating and doing investigations with my peers who are paranormal investigators. During the investigations, while I am communicating with Spirit, my messages are often validated by recordings picked up with their paranormal equipment.

During my twenties, I did not focus too much on my abilities except to realize that I could not deny that I had them. I thought and sometimes hoped that they would go away, but guess what? They did not. I was still very much in tune to the people and things going on around me, and I was still always wanting to help people more than anything else. This seemed to be my focus with every career I explored as well.

In my first job as a cosmetologist, I used my creativity doing hair, nails and makeup. This enabled me to help people with their self-confidence and well-being. I was also a retail manager, where I was dealing with people and helping them to look their best. After that I worked in an office setting where I was assisting many people with customer service. Owning my own cleaning business came next, where I helped people to have a clean and organized home.

Helping each other was also very common growing up in my tight-knit family. One of my closest relationships was with my paternal grandfather. He always helped everyone, from family to friends to strangers. This man had the biggest heart. What an awesome role model to have. At the time of his passing, I remember feeling such extreme hurt and loss. I thought to myself, "What would I do without him?" We had an extraordinary bond.

Soon after his death, he came to me one night in Spirit, giving me the message that I needed to let him go. He said he had to cross over to be with his loved ones on the other side, but he would always watch over me. This visit from him gave me such comfort because I somehow knew that he would never really leave me. This assured me that whether a loved one is in a physical body or crossed over into Spirit, their love never dies. I share this message that "love never dies" with all my clients to this day. A few years later, I was blessed when my son was born. My one job, the job I always wanted, being a Mom, had finally started. I could now understand the true meaning of unconditional love.

In my thirties, shortly after my divorce, I began to work with an extremely talented Psychic Advisor. She had predicted my divorce as well as many other things that all ended up coming true at various times. While working with her I would drive her to psychic parties, book her appointments, and advertise for her. We became very close friends, but she also became my mentor. I asked her many questions about my abilities as they began to develop more and more. She told me that I was highly intuitive. As my abilities grew stronger and more apparent, I began to acknowledge and accept them. I thought to myself, "I certainly do have a gift, but I will never read for people like she does." I watched the drain of energy and the time she put into helping others.

In my mind I was afraid to embrace being a reader. What would people think who knew me before as just Joann, friend, mom, business owner, but not a psychic medium?

Something I also found to be very interesting while working with my mentor was something called "Table Tipping." Table tipping is another method used to connect to Spirit. It offers sensory validation as people can see the table move and they can also feel the energy of Spirit when it comes through the table. As a group, everyone places their hands on a small card table asking simple questions directed toward their loved ones who have crossed. Spirit energy will actually move the table in a tipping motion, going through the alphabet and spelling out responses to questions. I found myself becoming a bit impatient during these sessions because I knew what Spirit was trying to say well before they had finished spelling out the word. I would end up blurting things out before the table had finished spelling, which was further validation that I was really connecting to and hearing Spirit.

I thought to myself, "I love being around new people and learning from them, and the stories of their lives are exciting too!" When I went to psychic parties, I would end up reading clients and picking up Spirit. Sometimes people would even show me photos and, as I found myself looking at the picture, I realized I was reading the person's soul through their eyes. The eyes are truly the window to the soul. When I look into someone's eyes, I see much deeper than just how they look on the outside. People never see themselves as someone else sees them. When we look at ourselves in the mirror, we are much more focused on our appearance-- we see our hair, body shape, etc. When others look into our eyes though, they may first notice that kind, friendly, caring nature. They have a capacity to look deeper into our soul than we can. I repeatedly said to myself, "I will never read like my Psychic Advisor mentor. It is too emotional. With my big heart, I will never be able to stay detached from others in need." Spirit did not care. Spirit and my Guides had a mind of their own. I had messages that needed to be delivered and advice and warnings that needed to be shared. I was really being pulled to read professionally, despite the voice inside my head that always fought so hard against it.

Then something strange occurred to me that made me think perhaps I should become a reader delivering messages to others. My step-grandmother passed away and a few days after her passing I was in my bed one night when I distinctly heard her voice. She was calling my name "Joann." I had never heard Spirit voices call out loud before this time. I had heard them in my head, but this was different. At first, I thought I was hearing things, but it was her voice. I knew that voice -- I had heard it all my life. I was naturally frightened, and I threw the sheet over my head. And then the sheet moved on its own. From that moment on, my abilities not only included sensing a presence and seeing and feeling Spirit but now also hearing Spirit voices out loud. I said to myself, "You must be going crazy, Joann." Tell no one or the men in the white coats are coming. Ha! I chalked it up to the stress I was going through at the time due to my divorce. It was simply my grandmother coming through to tell me, "It's all going to be ok." Just an important message I needed to hear from a loved one. When you are among the living, you only see what is in front of you and around you-- only what you can see with your eyes in the present moment -- but Spirit tells me that once you cross over, you see everything clearly.

Shortly after this interesting experience when Spirit spoke to me out loud, my son and I moved and once again my abilities heightened. I was now never ever alone! Spirits were with me all the time. I could see them, hear them, and feel their touch. It became more and more apparent to me that my ability was here to stay and getting stronger than ever! Nighttime was almost always a constant party in the Spirit world with a lot of Spirit activity around me. I spent most of my nights awake talking with Spirit, who were giving me messages for myself and other people. I began to think I had more friends on the other side than I had here amongst the living. I often still feel this way.

I can remember the night that I received a phone call from my mom telling me that her boyfriend had just passed away. My son and I had been very close to him. As I was consoling my son and trying to explain that his "Poppy" will always be right by his side, I actually saw him in Spirit. My mom's boyfriend was kneeling next to my son at the side of his bed. He said to me, "Joann, watch over him, as I will do the same." In some strange way I felt comfort at that moment.

What I have since learned by studying this world is that it is very common for Spirit to make one last visit to their loved ones before they cross over. This usually occurs within twenty-four to seventy-two hours of their passing. I often call this a "fly by." Still to this day Poppy will let me know that he is around by the distinct smell of his cigar smoke. Each Spirit has its own unique sign. This event confirmed to me, once again, that Spirit is among us, and the soul never truly dies.

I turned to my mentor for guidance because she had been doing this work for fifty years. I told her about all the things I was picking up and what was happening to me. I felt that I was truly becoming an open portal to the other side. She explained to me that I was getting very direct and clear messages from my Spirit Guides. Everyone is born with a Spirit Guide -- a soul who once lived in a physical body who walked a similar path as you are walking in this lifetime. This Spirit Guide will stay with you throughout your lifetime to help assist you through your life journey. The best way to communicate with them is to listen to your gut instinct. Your gut is never wrong!

My mentor confirmed that my energy and my abilities would continue to become stronger and more precise as I grew older. She urged me to pursue my abilities and to read clients because I could help many people along the way just as she had done. But she wanted me to ALWAYS remember that I live here on earth and not in the spirit world. She encouraged me to balance my time between reading clients and making time for myself. She told me that no one will ever understand the amount of energy it takes to read unless you are a reader yourself. She advised me that you must walk away from it from time to time or you will burn out. She knew I had a big heart and that people's needs were so important to me. She wanted to remind me that my needs were important too. She had walked in my shoes in this profession and was giving me very sound advice.

I finally surrendered! I began to read clients professionally. One of them happened to be a client named Cindy, who now works with me as a Meditation and Manifestation Instructor. I read her and connected with her loved ones. I felt peace while reading Cindy and thought to myself, "This woman has her own abilities and her own intuition. She could also bring peace and confidence to others." I could visualize her working beside me, and so I invited Cindy to work with me. She was quite surprised and caught a bit off guard, but guess who now works with me? I refer to Cindy as my "Lois Lane." When I receive premonitions or details about something, Cindy does the homework and validates the information I receive. We have had many laughs, and we still respond to each other with, "HOLY COW! How did you receive those messages?" The answer is always the same: Spirit Guides or a loved one

-- just depends on who is doing the talking that day.

Another special person I met along the way was Aleja. She had been a client of my Psychic Advisor mentor for almost twenty years. I would attend home parties she hosted for my Psychic mentor friend. I would always volunteer to drive as she served the best snacks. I remember being in her space and saying to myself, "Joann, she is very in tune, she can read!" I invited her to my home to talk. I read her, and guess what? She was very intuitive as well. Although she often second guesses herself, she can pick up on many things from Spirit. She certainly can feel Spirit. Aleja is very empathic which is only one of many reasons why she is such a good Reiki Practitioner. I invited her to work with me, and she also said yes. The rest is history. Aleja wears many hats as she is also the web designer and photographer for my business.

These women have both become my dear friends and confidantes, and I was fortunate enough to get them to work side by side with me. As a result, Psychic Treasures Unlimited was born! Together we will continue our "Healing of the Mind, Body & Soul."

I have learned so much over the years about the spiritual world. My Spirit Guides have taught me to trust their knowledge as they are very wise old souls. The advice I receive from them is right on the money. I have learned to trust in the Universe as it knows best and will deliver things in due time. For me, patience is not always my virtue. It's like having blind faith--you need to just trust that the Universe has a plan for each and every one of us. The Universe will point you in the direction you need to be in to help with life's lessons. Each situation you go through will help get you to your final destiny. It may be where you are living, the people you are connected to, or a particular situation.

Spirits who have crossed over have also taught me that love never dies. They will give you signs or acknowledgements that they are around to protect you or warn you about something. Loved ones come through in spirit to tell you that they are here with you and you are not alone.

A big lesson I have seen while consulting with clients, friends or family, is to learn not to be afraid to love. Sometimes we need to just get back up after falling out of the tree, brush ourselves off, and move on. We need to accept love from others as it is the driving force of one's soul. We need to understand that love can hurt at times, but not everyone showing or giving you love will hurt you. It's an emotion that all souls have, and one emotion that is the hardest to accept. Speaking for myself, I can honestly say it is much easier for me to give love than to accept it. This is a lesson I need to work on.

Spirituality is about something bigger than ourselves. It resonates in each and every one of us in different ways. Mine has grown so much by trusting in Spirit. I am someone who likes to be in control and I have had to learn that often I am not in the driver's seat. As I read and deliver messages for many, I truly have no control over what the message or answer to a question may be. Many people don't understand spirituality or don't want to learn about it, so they assume it is a type of religion, cult, or maybe even something evil. I can assure you through my studies and my ability to connect with Spirit that spirituality is none of those things. I would suggest taking the time to study spirituality and learn more about it. It could help you to understand that a soul exists whether in a physical body or as pure energy when someone passes. As time goes on and we continue to grow, we always learn new things. As our life evolves, so do our life lessons. We are going to make mistakes along this life journey from time to time and that is ok, as long as we learn from our mistakes and try hard not to repeat them.

I like to believe that life is not a destiny -- it's a journey -- so why not enjoy the ride? I know this holds true for myself. With every experience and obstacle, I have grown. I believe I am exactly where the Universe needs me to be, although I may not like it at times. My job as a reader on some days is to point out the obvious to my many clients, friends, and family that their answers are often right in front of them. You just need to look a little harder. I have often noticed that giving good advice over the years to others is easier than listening to it myself.

Many people will ask me, "How do you hear your Guides, how do you hear Spirit?" I tell them that I just hear it in my head. I can't really explain it in detail. It's a "knowing" I have in my mind and in my gut. I JUST KNOW! I will occasionally hear in audio sound Spirit calling my name or saying something. Many people will also ask me how I see my Guides or Spirit? I sometimes see them in the form of a white mist and at other times very vividly, just as if I were looking at a person. I often just simply feel their presence, whether it be male or female.

I share my ability with many. I have lost friends along the way, as some of my friends are still trying to figure out what happened to Joann before she became Joann the Psychic Medium. I can assure you that I am the same person, but now I am embracing my ability to receive messages that maybe those friends were not ready to hear. Many people think that having the ability of a Psychic Medium must be very cool and glamorous. They assume it must be exciting to be able to receive knowledge about life and to simply "know" so many things. Like anything else in life, it has its ups and downs.

I'll admit that there are times when I will not share that I am a reader. It is nice to sometimes just be Joann, with no one knowing I can communicate with spirit. I do ask myself at times, "Do these people want to be my friend, do they like me for me, or is it my ability that they like?" I do know that my role in this lifetime is to help people. This ability is a gift. It was incorporated into my genetics at birth. It was defined by study. I believe it was enhanced by receiving energy through my great-grandmother's touch. In whatever way I obtained it, it is quite real! I am the open portal through which Spirit can communicate. My ability, however, is not like a light switch. I cannot turn it off and believe me there are times when I wish I could.

I have had the pleasure of meeting many people and making many new friends on this journey including other readers, paranormal investigators, and clients. When I am able to share insight to help people, I have achieved success. It is not always easy delivering messages or predictions. My personality defines how I read. I am very honest -- I tell everyone if you don't want to know, then don't ask! I also let them know I don't know everything, but whatever message I receive I will deliver. Messages are not always positive, but they need to be heard just the same.

After all this time, when I am talking to a client, a family member, or even a friend, I still sometimes ask myself, "How did I just get that message? Where did it come from? Did I hear that? Did I just feel that? How did I see that?" Can you believe, after all these years, I still wonder to myself how I receive so many messages from Spirit? The tears, the hugs, and the validation I receive from so many makes me believe I am doing exactly what I am supposed to. I look forward to my continued journey on this path, alongside Cindy and

Aleja, meeting new people, discovering new things and helping others to heal their mind, body and soul.

CINDY

"Never underestimate the power of your mind. Positive thoughts garner positive results." ~Cindy

Throughout my life, I have been told that I possess a naturally calming and soothing presence. I have always felt other people's pain and had a strong desire to comfort those who were unhappy or hurting. From my earliest memories to the present day, being a caretaker was what I seemed to do best. One of my early memories of childhood was being around my grandfather, who was quite sick and very unhappy around anyone, especially children. Somehow, I found my way into his heart by simply spending time with him and making him smile. My family was amazed at the joy I brought to him. I was not going to accept him being alone and unhappy as an answer. I was determined to fix it. I have always been the empathic friend who has everyone coming to discuss their problems and to cry on my shoulder.

I always felt different somehow from other children. I was a chronic daydreamer. My imagination was vivid and always turned on. I had imaginary friends -- entire cities of them under the bushes in front of my house. I also had terrifying nightmares about all different things. I never watched much television, although I was drawn to The Ghost and Mrs. Muir, A Family Affair, Bewitched, and movies from Old Hollywood with scenes that somehow felt familiar. I would write creative stories and illustrate them for hours at a large desk that took up half my bedroom. I often wrote about and was drawn to stories of the past. I was interested in anything about Colonial Times, Medieval England and Ancient Egypt. I would read whatever books I could find about Henry VIII or Cleopatra and would fantasize about what it would be like to live their lives. I also loved stories about the supernatural or anything magical, but I did not like to watch or read anything that was frightening.

As a young child, I dreaded going to bed and I dreaded the dark due to recurring nightmares I had about strangers hiding out in our home. When I had these bad dreams, my poor father would guide me through every inch of our apartment, opening and inspecting every closet to assure me that nobody frightening was lurking anywhere. He would keep reassuring me, "See Cindy! There are no strange people here. Nobody is here but us."

To keep myself preoccupied, I remember actually moving pens and other small objects with my mind in order to stay focused on something besides the bad people I was imagining in my bedroom. I never thought much of the fact that I could do this. In my child's mind, I just figured that everyone could. I now know that this skill -- being able to move objects with your mind -- is referred to as "telekinesis." To me it did not have a label --it was simply my normal.

If you were a child of the seventies, you probably remember the "light as a feather" trick, a popular slumber party game where you would lie down and pretend with your mind that you were "light as a feather." Your friends would circle around you, each putting one finger under you, and when you felt the moment was right you would have them try to lift you up into the air. This was usually the point when the game failed because nobody could be budged. But when I played this game with my friends, they would watch in disbelief because I would rise into the air with virtually no effort at all. I would be lifted clear over their heads, each of them holding me with just one finger. I really believed that I was as light as a feather. I was convinced that I could be lifted high without any effort, and it would happen every time. I believe these early experiences were my training ground in first understanding the awesome unlimited power and potential of our minds.

Unlike other children, I had to work tirelessly to fit in and feel normal. What I really did not understand, above all, was what I perceived as children's lack of compassion and kindness. I grew up attending public school in New York City. The culture of children on the playground swing set and dodge ball corner was mean, overwhelming, and an energy that I simply did not understand. In a world where you can be anything, I wondered why children so often chose to be unkind? One day in school, a friend of mine who had cerebral palsy had his notebooks and three-ring binders knocked out of his arms by bullies and his papers deliberately kicked all over the hallway. I helped him to pick up every paper, tears streaming down my face, and I wondered why children could be so cruel.

I was sensitive and compassionate, always having empathy for the underdog and the underprivileged. My mama would say that I took in all the "strays." I listened to Pete Seeger albums and cried at the song "Puff the Magic Dragon." I was somber about the fact that everyone could not be as fortunate as me and that they could not have the love and kind family and financial security that I was so privileged to enjoy. I made friends with the homeless man that I passed each day on the street corner while walking to school, and my heart ached for him. Why was there not enough happiness to go around, and why did some people on earth seem to suffer so?

I often studied people and seemed to have a sense about their struggles and their hardships. I seemed to sense what emotions people were feeling. I also often had a gut instinct about whether people might have good or bad intentions.

As I was growing older, I found myself continuing to explore certain eras or time periods in history. I read The Little House on the Prairie series countless times. I felt that I had wandered those woods and I had lived in a log cabin on that prairie just like Laura Ingalls. I would ask my grandfather to take me to historical sites. I liked learning about them, and they always felt familiar and comfortable.

My grandmother's old house at Lake George in upstate New York also felt full of energy to me. I always sensed that someone was watching me, especially in the bedroom where I slept, but nobody was really there. I would stare at the old portraits of people on her wall and feel as if they were talking to me -- that I could familiarize with them and their life. I would sense how their lives in the era they lived had been so different from mine, yet they also somehow felt familiar. I could sense their struggles and hardships as if I was feeling their emotions. This would happen to me fairly often when I went into old places. Was I experiencing déjà vu?

I spent a great deal of time outside in nature, and I felt like I had a new lease on life when we moved from New York City to New Jersey where we suddenly had a yard, green grass, and trees. I would stare at the greenery for hours and spent so much time outdoors creating fairy villages out of sticks and rocks. I could never get enough. My dad would tease me because I was always running around outside barefoot. Being out in nature is something that I still crave today -- an activity that always soothes and restores me. I have always felt like I derive some kind of strength from the earth.

The teenage years brought my first solid encounter with Spirit. I went on a trip with my family to an island with a colorful history and a quaint old fishing village. We stayed overnight in a very old home and I was in bed with a younger sibling. In the middle of the night, an apparition that seemed to have a female face, and appeared to be floating, came and sat on the bed. She was wearing old-fashioned clothing, the outline of which could be seen. The Spirit casually remarked that her husband had gone to sea and she was eagerly awaiting his return. I could hear this vision talking to me and I was freaking out! Her voice sounded strange, her language like nothing I had ever heard. When she first entered, I was just waking up out of dream state, but I was soon wide awake, and she was still there and definitely not a part of any dream! I knew this apparition was real and not a figment of my imagination. I truly did not know what to do or what to make of this experience. All I could think about as I sat there in bed, frozen, looking at her through the slits of my eyes while pretending to be asleep, was that my sibling could not wake up and see this.

Shortly after this incident, I started experiencing a kind of night terror in my sleep which I now know is referred to as sleep paralysis. This occurs when a person wakes up before the REM stage is complete. It can happen to anyone, but many intuitive people report it as a common experience. I would wake up in a frozen state of helplessness, unable to move or scream, feeling like an elephant was on my chest. I would fight so hard to move and break out of the spell I seemed to be under that held me frozen. These events were so frightening and confusing. I still experience sleep paralysis to this day, and it is always terrifying.

At the time, I naturally connected this experience to the other strange things that had been happening to me, such as seeing apparitions and experiencing déjà vu, and I turned to my parents describing all of these events. My family was not necessarily open to the concept of Spirits as an explanation for anything, and my mom chalked it up to the nail polish fumes that she assumed must be going to my head when I painted my nails right before bed. I figured she must be right. Even though these experiences were happening to me quite often, I learned to ignore and suppress them for the most part.

When I entered college, I became much more independent and felt free to explore new things, including the world of Spirit that I had always been attracted to. I began to study all the psychic phenomena that I did not fully understand. I described the psychic experiences I had had my entire life to an important and open-minded friend for the first time. There was also a brilliant and ever curious student who lived in my dorm complex who experimented with levitating and hypnotizing me. Through hypnosis, he took me back to a prior life that I had lived, and I experienced my childhood birthday party from that lifetime while under hypnosis. I apparently became very childlike during the session -- my voice changed, and I expressed all the emotions that I had experienced as a child in that previous lifetime during my birthday party. This was the one and only time that I have had any kind of past life experience under hypnosis. I think it would be interesting to do it again with a professional hypnotist. In college, I suddenly felt free to pursue these various interests for the first time, and as a result, I became much more in tune to Spirit during these years.

Around this time in my life, I also took several trips to England that were transformative and played a key role in my awareness of spirit energy. I sensed spirit energy everywhere I went in England, and everything seemed heightened compared to my sensibilities in the United States. I could feel the energy of a Spirit in my boyfriend's apartment in Cambridge, and it felt like the energy of someone in a jealous rage. I could feel the deep emotions of bitterness and fear when I entered the Tower of London. When I visited a small isolated Abbey in northern England that had been inhabited by monks, I could feel their somber emotions. I also had the feeling of fear while standing in the great halls of Hampton Court. I was not sure why I kept feeling overwhelmed by fear. The friend I was with at the time suggested that perhaps I was picking up the emotions of one of Henry VIII's wives who had been removed from this castle to be thrown into jail and beheaded during the Middle Ages. There seemed to be restless energy all over England, and I felt that I was somehow getting in tune to the emotions of others or of past events. People in England were also much more open to the concept of ghosts and Spirits, which was very different from my experience with most people in the United States. This in turn made me more open-minded about all the experiences I had had throughout my life.

I never mentioned much about all this to my boyfriend who was studying in England. I thought he would think I was crazy. Therefore, I was so surprised when he called me before he was finished with the school year to tell me that he had decided to leave Cambridge early and not finish up his degree. He later told me that he could absolutely swear that a Spirit had been haunting his apartment there, and that the day he left this Spirit had tried to push him down the stairs as he was on his way out the door. This had to be the same Spirit I had felt every time I stayed there with him! I still, to this day, believe that this nasty Spirit's presence was part of the reason why my boyfriend packed up and left England early, without obtaining his degree.

I graduated college and I entered the corporate world on Wall Street. I found this very unfulfilling, so shortly after I was married, I left that job to earn a graduate degree and become a teacher. I suddenly felt satisfied and fulfilled and believed that teaching was my calling. I then raised three children of my own. At this point in my life, I spent a long stretch of time ignoring, suppressing and burying my own intuition and connection to Spirit. My family did not really believe in the Spirit world or want to hear much about it. I feel that my intuition started to diminish as a result. I do believe that it is like a muscle- if you do not regularly tune into your intuition, it tends to weaken.

Throughout this time, however, I kept a small hand in this world that was always familiar and comfortable to me. I pursued my interest in paranormal investigations with a fellow computer teacher who was also my mentor. He always wanted me to come with him on his ghost hunts with his students because we had great success together in connecting with the spirit world. We went to an historic site in Princeton one day, and when I pressed my hand to the glass window of this old home while standing outside, I felt so much energy run through me. The next moment, my friend was getting all kinds of audio coming through his paranormal equipment. Through his headphones he could hear voices saying, "Help me!" clear as day. I still do many paranormal investigations with him to this day, along with Joann and Aleja.

I also received many premonitions, which is a psychic ability referred to as Claircognizance. There were certain things I just knew that would give me a pit in my stomach. For example, when George W. Bush was elected to the Presidency for his first term, I called my friends from college and told them, "I have to tell someone this information so that I have a witness. I am having a premonition that we are going to enter a war with Iraq under President Bush. This is a premonition, very clear and strong, and I just feel the need to tell someone." September 11th had not yet occurred, our country did not seem to have any reason to enter into a war, so my friends just thought I was crazy. But I was learning to trust my intuition and premonitions, and to verbalize to friends and family what I was feeling and what I was anticipating was to come.

I also had a vision of the entire September 11th tragedy the night before it occurred. Early on the morning of 9/11, after I had had this very disturbing vision, I told a close friend about the premonition. I happened to be going to Boston the next weekend to see my sister, and I told this friend that I was glad I was not flying to Boston on this upcoming trip, but rather driving there. When asked why, I stated that I had had a very clear vision during the night, and I felt that something awful was about to happen with planes being hijacked and crashing into buildings. I could not tell from the vision that the setting was the World Trade Center, but I saw buildings up in smoke, I saw planes exploding into them, I saw people jumping out of the windows of the buildings, and I had a vision of a plane crashing in a field. I described all of this to him early that morning, and he called me later that day in disbelief, after all the events had unfolded very much like I had described.

I had several friends who died that day in the World

Trade Center, and my kids went to the same preschool as the children of Todd Beamer, the hero who said, "Let's Roll" and took down the plane in Pennsylvania on that fateful day. I sometimes wonder if my connection to so many people who perished that day is the reason why I saw these events unfold so clearly in my mind's eye before they played out in reality. Was I receiving a message?

Shortly after this, my biological father passed away suddenly. I had not spent very much time with him during my lifetime because he and my mom divorced when I was very young. I believe my biological father's death was the event that really activated my intuition and also some new abilities.

I was pregnant with my third child when he died, but his Spirit was suddenly in my bedroom, tapping me awake every night and really startling me. I was now clearly feeling Spirit touch, which is referred to as Clairtangency, and sensing Spirit presence when it was around me, which is called Clairsentience. This was occurring more and more frequently. I don't know how, but I simply knew his soul, and that this energy in my bedroom at night was my biological father. I could feel his sadness and his deep regret that he was not able to spend much time with me during our life together on earth. His energy was so sad, it made me cry! My empathic pathways were opening up along with my intuitive abilities, my sense of just knowing certain things.

When Joann later connected with my biological father in Spirit, he revealed to her that my abilities have come to me genetically through his family line. These were people that both he and I had never known, as he had been adopted and never came to know his biological family during his lifetime.

I did not tell my family about these experiences until one night when my father's Spirit woke me up once again, as had happened many nights in a row, tapping firmly on my leg while I was sleeping in bed. As I arose, his energy seemed to move off into the bathroom that was situated adjacent to the bedroom. The next moment, the pipes in the bathroom were banging so loud it sounded like pots and pans clanging together. The noises startled us, and I sat bolt upright in bed exclaiming, "What is that?! What the heck is that noise? Who is in the house?" At that point I broke down crying, sensing my dad, Jerry, who was here in Spirit and was so very sad! At that moment, I went into the bathroom and sat on the edge of the bathtub, six months pregnant, and started the first of many conversations with my biological father who was now in Spirit. I spoke to him out loud, telling him that I felt his sadness, that everything was ok, that I knew he loved me, that I loved him as well, and that I would see him one day on the other side. Then I asked him to please stop waking me up every night and crashing around the house because he was frightening us!

A few years after this, I suffered the most devastating

loss of my life, the death of my sixty-one-year-old mother from ALS (Lou Gehrig's disease). My mother and I had a unique bond that is difficult to describe. She was my best friend, my rock, and my world. Her illness had been extremely difficult, and I was not with her the night that she died. I believe this was the way she chose it to be. Sometimes people wish to be alone when they pass, rather than having their loved ones around, as they don't want their passing to be hard on the ones they leave behind.

I had three young children, one just two years old, and I had been with my mom constantly as we knew she was in her final days. I spoke to the hospice nurses that day and said that I wanted to get home to my children for just one night. They told me to go. They said, "Your mother is very strong, and people die the way they live. She will probably hang on for another day. Go home to your children and return tomorrow." I went home to my children, but in the middle of the night that night, I sat up in bed as I immediately sensed my mother's presence in my bedroom. I said, "Good-bye dear mama. I know you just passed." The next minute my cousin called from my parent's house to tell me that my mom had died moments earlier. I was already crying when I received the phone call, and my response to her was, "Yes, I know." This same type of thing happened to me when my grandparents died as well, where their energy came through to me and I knew they had just passed. Also, these loved ones all presented themselves to me in my dreams shortly after their deaths, looking healthy and happy once again, seeming to assure me that they were now ok.

When I arrived at my mama's home just after her death, the hospice nurses told me that several birds had been around her window the entire last day that my mother was here on earth. They told me that, from their experience, this was common, and the nurses believed that the birds represent your loved ones coming to cross you over when you are dying. They stated that the transition often seems to be very close at hand when they see birds arrive, and my mom's death had been no different.

I was sitting in a chair in my bedroom a few days later crying my eyes out, talking to my dear mother in Spirit when I said out loud to her, "I need to feel your touch. I just want you to hug me one more time." Then I became very surprised because suddenly I felt her presence and she was holding me, with not a doubt in my mind about what I was feeling. It was just as if she were there in physical form. I started to laugh, and cry, and honestly freak out because this was yet another situation that was not understandable or explainable to me. These experiences I was having with the spirit world had magnified tremendously with the death of my two parents. But their deaths and what happened subsequently had also revealed to me an important and very comforting truth: the soul is eternal. It was undeniable to me based upon these experiences that my parents' souls had continued on after their physical shells were gone.

Shortly after my mom's passing, we had a memorial service for her in Maryland where my brother lived. As we were driving down for the service, we saw three billboards with large frogs on them. My mom had adored frogs. They were very special to her, and she had a large collection of porcelain and crystal frogs. Seeing these billboards on the way down, it seemed like she was communicating with us from the spirit world. When I went to sleep that night, I said, "Mama, I know you are with me here. I have felt your presence with me all day. If you are here and you are happy, please give me a sign." That night, in the middle of the night, my iPod turned on by itself and started blasting the song with the following lyrics, "I was born, born, born, born to be alive." I never even knew that song was on my device and had never listened to it! Much like the frogs on the billboards, this was yet another strong sign from my mama in Spirit.

During my mother's final days, there was a voice inside my head that kept repeating, "Ask and you shall receive," and I was seeing frogs everywhere I looked. My mama did not spend much time during her life thinking about where you went once you crossed over, and she never liked discussing my intuitive abilities or this spirit world that I seemed to be immersed in. Therefore, discussions about her impending death and what might happen afterward were not easy conversations for us. But I took some time with her one morning and I opened the subject. I told her that after she passed, I wanted her to send me a sign in the form of a frog. As I said before, my mother absolutely loved and had a special relationship with frogs. She surrounded herself with them and she loved to listen to them sing at night. I told her that when she sent me a frog sign, I did not want her to mess around. I wanted it to be a big huge frog, and when I saw this frog, I would know it was from her. I did not want there to be a doubt in my mind that this was mama's frog.

One evening around dusk, I was taking garbage out to the trash can in the garage. The garage door was wide open that night. As I approached the can, I noticed sitting in the middle of the garage door jamb the biggest bullfrog I had ever seen in my life! I had never seen a frog on my property before this, let alone a bullfrog. "Hi mama!" I exclaimed excitedly. I called all my children out to the garage to see the frog as they all knew that I had asked for it. This frog sat there and let us pet it, and it looked like it was smiling. I could feel the energy flowing from this frog into my hands, and I knew in that moment that my mama was ok.

Another loss I experienced shortly after my mom's death was the loss of my grandmother, with whom I was very close. I was sleeping in her farmhouse one night right after she died when I had another experience with Spirit. I found myself looking at the doorway when I saw my grandmother standing in it, just as I would see her standing there if she were alive. I began to have a conversation with her. Was I dreaming or was I awake? To this day, I am still not sure. I could hear my grandmother's voice talking to me. As I sat up, she seemed to disappear. The door actually slammed shut, and I could hear footsteps pacing for a little while afterward. I laid back down very quickly, and then I continued to hear what sounded like footsteps pacing in the hallway outside my bedroom.

The next morning my aunt, who had been sleeping downstairs in the bedroom just below mine, asked me how I had slept the night before. "Oh, just fine!" I fibbed. She said, "Really? Are you sure? There was an awful lot of commotion and noises and something that sounded like footsteps pacing back and forth last night. It sounded like you were busy up there having a party!" I had never physically left my bed the entire night, and I was the only other person sleeping in the house that evening. I just smiled at her and shrugged my shoulders.

Since I was now connecting to both of my deceased parents and my grandma in ways that I could not understand, and because I missed them and wanted to seek their guidance, I started to search for a talented Psychic Medium who might be able to assist me. My research led me to a critically acclaimed Psychic Advisor who assisted and mentored me for a time and answered so many of my questions about what was happening to me. This connection then led me to a meeting with Joann, whose important role as a Medium would be to connect me to my loved ones in Spirit in a very concrete way.

When I prepped for the appointment with Joann that morning, I put on a very special diamond necklace that I had inherited from my mother just after her death. I spoke to my mother out loud while getting dressed that morning in my home. During this conversation, I pointed to the necklace and said out loud, "Mama, if you come through today in my Medium reading, I want you to acknowledge this necklace that I am wearing, and then I will know that it is you." It was wintertime, so I purposely put on a turtleneck that covered the necklace completely. It was not visible at all. I then made my way to Joann's office for my appointment.

When Joann opened the door to let me in, she immediately started pointing to her neck, saying, "Are you wearing a necklace under that turtleneck? A female Spirit is standing right behind you and talking to me about a necklace that you are wearing." From that first amazing moment when I arrived, the reading continued to go very well!

My father was getting re-married the next day, and my mother communicated through Joann that she knew my dad was getting married and that she would be at the wedding in Spirit. She told me to look for signs of her presence. When I drove into the venue the next day for the wedding with my brother and sister, there were three deer standing in the driveway, blocking our entrance. We were three children in the car, and there were three deer in the driveway, and we all just stared at each other for several minutes. My mom had also said there would be someone in a very ugly dress at the wedding. There was, and it made me laugh! During my reading, my mom also provided countless stories and pieces of information to prove her identity and to show her love. It was a transformative experience.

My mom and dad had buried a sister of mine years earlier. She had been born with a life-threatening tumor on her head, and she died about a month after she was born. Her death had been devastating to my mother. She seemed to never get over the loss during her lifetime. But when my mama came through that day, she let me know that she was reunited with my sister on the other side. She said that my sister had been the one to greet and cross her over when she passed. Although it was so painful for my mom to lose my sister during her lifetime, their souls were reunited on the other side. My sister had had the important role of helping to cross my mother over. Once again, this revealed to me that all souls are eternal and there are no permanent good-byes.

I also went to the reading that day to discuss my own experiences with Spirit that were becoming more frequent and which were so confusing to me. Joann sensed something spiritual from me during my reading. Before I left that day, she said, "I believe you are intuitive and have something to offer, and perhaps you should think about working with me." This was the strangest thing in the world to me. I had never dreamed of or imagined working with a Psychic Medium to use my own intuition or abilities to help others. I went home that afternoon thinking I would probably never see Joann again. But she called me again a few weeks later asking if I had given any thought to working with her. I had lived so many years trying to suppress my abilities, but now I had found someone who was actually encouraging them, who was telling me that these abilities were real and even useful. She assured me that it was ok to foster them, and that they were a positive thing.

Joann finally gave me the eyes and ears to make sense of all the things that were happening to me that I did not understand. Since that moment, Joann has served as a mentor, helping to broaden my horizons and foster my abilities. This led to an indelible friendship and the beginning of our path in forming a business together.

Joann gave me yet another beautiful gift by allowing my mom and biological dad to communicate to me from the spirit world. When they first started communicating through Joann, they never seemed to be getting along. They had been divorced during their lives, so I guess this was not a surprise. I could sometimes feel their tension, and Joann was certainly seeing and describing it as well. When she connected with my mom, my dad would leave, and vice versa. I was getting a bit frustrated with the situation, so one day I spoke to them out loud while I was taking a shower. This may sound funny, but Spirit always hears us. When you speak to your loved ones out loud, they do receive your messages. Joann has taught me that it is easier to make a connection to Spirit when near water because water attracts Spirit. While in the shower, of all places, we can often communicate and receive downloads of information from Spirit. This still happens to me to this day.

Therefore, while I was showering one morning, I stated out loud to my mom and my biological father that I was disappointed in their petty fighting. I reminded them that they had made me out of love, and that I wished for them to get back to that place of love. I was going through some very stressful times in my life, and I told them that I really could use their unified support to help me from the other side. I never told Joann about this shower conversation, but she called me later that afternoon from her car. I picked up the phone and she said, "Cindy, I am not sure why, but I am being asked to deliver a message to you. I have been running errands, and I just looked in my rear-view mirror because I can see the Spirits of your mother and your biological dad in the back seat of my car. Your mother just took his hand and lifted their two hands clasped together into the air, so that I can see them holding hands in the rear-view mirror. Your mother asked me to give you the message that yes, indeed, she and your dad did make you out of love and that they remember that love and have come together for you." I immediately started to cry, and when I explained to Joann what I had asked them for while taking a shower that morning, she almost drove off the road in her own surprise. Ask and you shall receive.

Joann wanted to introduce me to her friend Aleja who also had intuitive ability. I will never forget one of our early meetings when Joann brought Aleja to my home. Aleja sat in my dining room and sensed a Spirit who had been there for a while, and who I also felt was there. We sat at the dining room table and Aleja became overwhelmed with sadness and was very adamant about wanting to explain what she was feeling and seeing. Her eyes began to fill up as she was sensing a great deal of sadness and tears around me and my family. Her intuition turned out to be spot on because shortly after that day my life turned upside down. My marriage was broken up by divorce and that home was sold a short time later. During this upheaval I did indeed experience great sadness and many tears. Aleja had sensed all of this on that day when she had come to my home. From that point on, Joann, Aleja and I began working together on a regular basis. A real connection between the three of us was beginning to form.

At that time, as my personal life was turning upside down, my own healing became very important. In the last several years, I have endured the breakup of my marriage, three relocations, and various other crises that occur while raising three children in a single parent household. Somewhere along the line, while desperately attempting to stay focused and calm in the midst of my chaos, I began to incorporate the practice of Meditation into my daily life. I started to attend classes, listened to any Meditation recording I could get my hands on, and studied and absorbed everything I could about this ancient practice. I discovered that I could truly ease my mind, tap into my intuition, and regulate my emotions with a daily practice of Meditation, and it became very important at this stressful time in my life.

Meditation also taught me the great benefits of

gratitude and positive thinking, which led me to start studying the Law of Attraction and the practice of Manifestation. I learned that we have the ability to bring things that we desire into our lives with focus, positivity and certain tools and visualization practices. I put this practice of Manifestation into effect with great results in my own life. I started to see the glass as half full rather than half empty with everything going on in my life, but most importantly I started to turn a lot of things in my life around for the better.

I will never regret the difficult times I went through during my divorce. I was forced to face many fears and I was forced to live a very different lifestyle than I had ever been used to, and all of these experiences taught me the very important trait of humility. This was a trait I had not exhibited much before this time in my life, and humility was a very important thing for me to learn. This is a lesson that I work hard to continue to learn every day.

Having the skills to quiet your mind, to stay in charge of your emotions, and to remain grateful and positive in the midst of chaos are some of the most important, healthy and beneficial abilities you could ever master. During this time I helped a very special friend who suffers from PTSD, due to his experiences surviving 9/11, by teaching him meditation skills and providing him with some of my recordings. I also helped my special needs brother to relax by listening to these audio meditation recordings. I made a special recording for my aunt who was passing, to help her transition to the other side in greater peace.

I sat down to speak with Joann about the positive results I had had after teaching these practices and providing recordings to people in my life. She said to me, "Cindy, I really think you need to teach Meditation and Manifestation professionally. So many clients I read could benefit from this." Meditation is also one of the most important tools anyone can use to connect to their inner world and develop their own intuition, which I had been doing myself. I had finally found my niche! With my life-long desire to help and comfort others, this was a perfect fit for me! I studied and obtained certifications, I recorded a series of original Meditations in a professional studio, and I was ready to help people in need. I was on my way! I look forward to everything the future will bring me, working with Joann and Aleja, and helping all of the people I have yet to meet along this journey!

ALEJA

"Everything happens for a reason." ~Aleja

My story is different from Joann's and Cindy's because they each seemed to know they had a gift from a very young age and yet grew up with parents who did not have an understanding or belief in the "spiritual world." I, on the other hand, am the direct opposite. My mother was a tarot card reader, palm reader, Psychic Medium, and clairvoyant, so I grew up in an environment of understanding paranormal experiences.

I can always remember friends and family both near and far seeking out my mom for her "gifted advice." It didn't even seem to matter whether or not they were skeptics or believers. They all valued her advice and would seek her out, looking for a peek into what could be lying ahead based on the current path they were on.

Regardless of their belief or disbelief, each time she gave advice she left them in awe. One of the last "predictions" I can remember her giving me was a time when we were with my daughter, who was in diapers and still crawling around on the floor, when out of the blue my mom said, "She is going to grow up to be a nurse." I never told a single solitary soul what she had told me. I sealed it in my memory bank and locked it away for years. I wanted to wait and watch my daughter grow up and see what choices she would make for herself. Long story short, guess what career path my daughter chose for herself? Nursing. Looks like my mom was right in her prediction twenty + years later, which is only one of many.

As you can see, the psychic and paranormal worlds were my normal growing up. It's a part of my chemical makeup and my DNA – a foundation of who I am today. There is literally no other way to explain it. There wasn't an introduction or a gradual transition into this world. I was just born into it. There was no denying it.

As a matter of fact, my parents told me that when I was born, I was born with a "body veil." Normally if a child is born with a veil, it's over their face. Mine was a "full body veil" which is not just unusual, but I have been told is even more significant. It is the belief to some that being born with a veil is an indication of being born with psychic gifts. The veil is actually a membrane called a caul.

It is only recently, when I decided to do a little more

research to further understand my spiritual gifts, that I learned what this really signifies. What I discovered about people who are born with a veil was truly shocking. I had never really given much thought to the fact that there were others like me, and never enough to look for documentation or confirmation. What I discovered was that people born with a veil, when they enter adulthood, seem to have commonalities. To name just a few, caulbearers or people born with a veil, have a natural empathic ability, can possess a healing touch, and have a natural ability to perform remote healings and, oddly, experience nose bleeds. My mouth was practically hanging open. There it was, totally unexpected, staring back at me from the page I was reading! Each of these things described who I am and have always been- the "healing touch", for example, is probably why I found a calling in Reiki healing. When I discovered Reiki, it hit me that it was something I needed to do. I immediately connected to it. It was like it had touched my soul and my soul was smiling at me telling me YES, this is the path you need to follow. However, being empathic or having a healing touch were things I didn't discover about myself until later. Learning this for myself has been a lifelong process.

I didn't grow up having "a knowing" that I was any of these things. Discovering my psychic gifts has been a lifelong journey of search and discovery to learn what gift I have that many psychics I'd encountered growing up kept insisting I had. Until I made these discoveries as an adult, I always wondered could they have all been wrong?

There had never been anything I was able to plug myself into. I didn't have loved ones come to visit me in the middle of the night sharing messages with me. I didn't have out of body experiences or have psychic visions that later were discovered to be predictions of the future. I didn't have lucid dreams. I wasn't able to pick up a deck of tarot cards and read someone's future or look into a crystal ball and have a bunch of messages download into my brain to share with others. Every time I'd been told I had a gift, it was all very vague. No one ever told me what to look for, how to develop it or what direction to go in. Only that it was important that I learn to develop it.

Looking back, I had never even thought to ask any questions. Instead, I became frustrated with my search. I didn't know where to begin to look or even how. I had no idea what I was looking for. Where was I supposed to start? I was always hoping for a sign. I was always looking for a sparkle that I could see with my eyes or hear like chimes, or that one thing that stood out and just called me saying, "Here I am! Over here. I am what you are looking for, develop me." Something, anything at all. That never seemed to happen. So started my lifelong journey and search to shed light on my childhood and everything I had been told about my spiritual gifts.

Where I grew up, not only was the paranormal normal for me, but so was playing in cemeteries. The house I grew up in was on a truck route, across the street from not one cemetery, but TWO! There was a trucking company up the street and next to our house was an open field and woods sat behind us. We didn't have many neighbors, but there was a home on each of the cemetery grounds where the groundskeepers lived.

There wasn't a whole lot in my neighborhood other than dead people! There was very little traffic to worry about so I could play in the roads of the cemeteries. You wouldn't think for a kid there would be a lot of entertainment there, but for me there was. I would bike ride, roller skate, have picnics with my sister, play house, pull my Barbies in their cars and much more.

Playing in the cemeteries never got old. Even when I got older, playing hide and go seek became popular when my friends came over. I'd take them into my playgrounds, the cemeteries, especially at night. There were LOTS of tombstones to hide behind. We would have teams since no one would want to be alone and, of course, this involved us jumping out at one another. Not to mention someone would always hum the tune to Friday the 13th when Jason was expected to pop out. As though being in the cemetery at night wasn't scary enough.

I recall a time in middle school when I had been playing with a friend of mine in the creepy graveyard. We had been bike riding and peered into an abandoned church that was right in the center of the graveyard, when I looked down and saw the oddest looking plastic toy. It was the strangest looking thing I'd ever seen. It had the head of a bird and the body of what I believed to be a seal. I picked it up, put it in my jacket pocket, and then zipped the pocket to take it home and show my mom to see if maybe she knew what it was. I went on my way and finished playing with my girlfriend until it was curfew. When I got home to show my mom this toy, it was missing! There was nothing there and there were no holes in my pocket that it could have fallen from. It was the first thing I looked for when I noticed it was missing. Even though I had nothing to show, I told my mom about what had happened. We thought nothing of it until much later.

This incident prompted me to start having terrible nightmares. This reminded me of vivid memories of having bad dreams when I was very young. The dreams or nightmares I had when I was less than eight years old would wake me up in the middle of the night feeling so scared that I couldn't get out of my bed fast enough. There was ALWAYS someone in the dreams chasing me or following me, which is very creepy to anyone, let alone to an elementary school aged child. Thankfully, when I'd have those bad dreams, my mom was a night owl and she'd always be awake watching television in the living room. I'd hang out with her until I was so sleepy my eyes wouldn't stay open anymore and then I'd go back to bed. This new resurgence of nightmares and bad dreams felt like déjà vu.

During this time my mom was introduced to a nice woman in the neighboring town who was a psychic and owned a florist shop. I had shared in detail my bad dreams with my mom and, without my knowledge, she shared them with the psychic florist who came to cleanse our house of any negative or unwanted spirits that may be taking up residence in the house that could be contributing to the bad dreams I was having. I didn't know this until weeks later when my mom asked me if I was still having the dreams. It was at that moment that I realized they had stopped without me even noticing. That's when my mom revealed that she had the psychic florist come to do a house cleansing when I was in school.

Interestingly, my mother had also been advised to destroy her very old Ouija board because it could be a portal that would allow uninvited spirits into the house. It was important for her to destroy the board, and not just throw it away, because it is said if you don't destroy a Ouija board to get rid of it then it will find its way back to you. Therefore, she destroyed her Ouija board and I never saw it again. I can remember seeing this board on our kitchen table surrounded by people asking questions as I stood by watching the planchette move around the board spelling out answers to their questions. You would think that maybe I would have learned not to play with Ouija boards after this, but I didn't.

In high school, when my one cousin and his neighbor would come over, we would go into the creepiest of the two cemeteries and sit on top of the graves using a Ouija board to communicate to the "people" below us. Of course, I kept in mind what the psychic florist advised, but she never said not to use one, just not to own one. I did have limitations though. I refused to have one in my house, in my car, or on my property. However, if it was not my board and not in or near my house or car, why not, right? So we did use the Ouija. Numerous times. Nothing significant ever really happened using Ouija in the cemeteries, but I did have a significant experience when using one somewhere else.

Going against my rule, because I decided that rules are meant to be broken, I had a girlfriend come over to my apartment with her Ouija board only hours after one of my cousins had suddenly passed away. The circumstances of his passing left us with some questions. My girlfriend and I thought maybe communicating with him through the use of the Ouija board would give us answers. Losing a loved one is never easy and often leaves you with questions. So we set out to get the truth directly from the horse's mouth. We had our white candle lit and we sat at my kitchen table and opened the board asking for my cousin.

It took no time at all. The entire apartment filled up with an indescribable energy that was so strong it almost felt like it would light up. The Ouija Board started going frantic, circling letters of the alphabet that spelled out, "Tell my mom I love her," then went through all his living siblings expressing his love to them and me, my parents.... it was UH-May-ZING! From the feel of the energy that filled the apartment (every nook and cranny), we both knew it was him. There was no doubt. This experience was the complete opposite of what people warned you about. This was a positive experience and quite remarkable -- once in a lifetime. Unfortunately, it all came to an abrupt end when my husband at the time came walking in. As soon as he opened the door, the energy disappeared as fast as a bubble burst in the wind, which more than likely was because our attention was redirected to my husband rather than to the Ouija board. The connection was lost. My girlfriend and I tried to get him back to finish but we were unsuccessful. We had our moment and our moment had passed.

I have always felt there was a lot more he wanted to say -- more messages he needed to communicate at that time. I have burned candles and have always hoped he is at peace now and that we didn't interrupt his transition. With all the readings I have had it wasn't until just now writing this that I thought to myself, "Why haven't I ever asked, Joann?" Or other readers I've crossed paths with before her? After all, Joann is one of the best, most accurate and gifted readers I have ever had the pleasure of knowing. She is a great friend to those she holds dear as well.

Having roots in the paranormal world, I have come across many types of readers. There are a couple of reads I've had that stand out in my mind. One was from a woman that I believe was recommended to my mom and she was a channeler. It was during her reading that "Spirit" apologized to me through her messages for the bad dreams I had had as a child. She said that those dreams were a result of my previous life not being shed completely before being born again into this life. I was told that those dreams were memories that hadn't been erased from my previous life and "Spirit" was sorry for the fear and stress I felt during that time.

Another experience came from a man who was not a reader, but someone who did past life regression through hypnosis. This experience was an eye-opener for me. This was when I started seeing how we are all connected. On the day of my appointment, the hypnotist had me sit in a recliner chair where I lounged back and had my feet up. I am not sure why I did this, but I remember thinking that it wasn't even going to work and started to laugh. He completely ignored my laughter and started the hypnosis process. It was almost like a guided meditation where he had me focus on parts of my body one at a time and had me relax them. He started with my feet and worked his way up to my head. By the time he walked me through the relaxation process and had me open my third eye. It was as though the chair had opened up and swallowed me. The relaxation that I felt was like no other. My body felt heavy as it sank into the chair. The feeling I experienced during hypnosis was a feeling I had never experienced again to this day. I was able to hear and know what was going on around me, but also had the feeling of almost being asleep. He continued on by guiding me to imagine myself walking up a flight of stairs. Once I reached the top of the stairs, he told me I'd see doors. Each door represented a life. The one I was meant to open would have a light around it. I was to walk up to that door and walk through. When I did this, it was like stepping through the closet in the movie Narnia. I stepped back in time and was in another place that was all very familiar to me.

Once I was through the door completely, he had me walk through what was my home during that previous life to look around and peer out the windows. When I looked out the windows, I was able to see that the house was sitting on a hill that faced a dirt road where the mode of transportation was horse and wagon and the women wore dresses. On the other side of the road were trees. It was quite beautiful. Peace and contentment was the energy I remembered feeling from this life. My home was well manicured and tidy, warm and inviting --very similar to how I strive for my current home to be to visitors in this life.

I was deaf in that past life, which impacted me being able to speak. My way of communicating was through the use of sign language. This explains my obsession with sign language in this current lifetime after being introduced to it in middle school. I learned to finger sign the alphabet, taught my friends and later taught my daughter words and short phrases, which we still use to this current day. When in middle school signing was how we were able to talk to one another without anyone else knowing what it was we were saying.

It is my belief that our fears, motivations, likes, dislikes, and connections to other people are a direct result of past lives we've lived. Ironically, while winding things up in writing my contribution to this very book, I developed mild to moderate hearing loss for medically unexplained reasons and am now wearing a hearing aid, which could very well be the connection to my past life. Is this coincidence or is this just something I've carried over from a previous life?

During the past life regression, I remember the furniture in my former home being made of a medium-colored wood, possibly red oak, dark maple, or cherry. My bed was a four-poster bed and was made with a white bedspread that was very similar, if not identical, to a vintage chenille bedspread. This explains the obsession I had with getting a four-poster bed when my husband (at the time) and I moved in together in this lifetime. The rule I had with him was no bed frame until I was able to find a very specific four-poster bed to accommodate our mattress.

As my past life regression session was nearing the end, the hypnotist directed me to fast forward to my final days of that life. Interestingly, I saw my caretaker and I saw myself lying in a bed that was dressed with sheets and a blanket, all in white. The hypnotist asked me if the person was someone I knew in this current life. Without hesitation, I knew my caretaker in that life is my sister in this life. It wasn't the color of her hair, the shape of her body, her body language or even her personality that I was able to identify with. It was the energy of her soul that was the identifier for me, that I so clearly was able to relate to now. It was a fascinating experience and I would definitely do it again.

Many years later, I had visuals of another past life while I was cooking dinner one evening after work. The vision was of me doing that same activity, but in a previous life with children around me helping to prepare the meal. It certainly wasn't like being under hypnosis because it was more of a flashback moment into that prior life -- very similar to having a random memory when you are sitting alone or driving home from work. I didn't get an opportunity to walk around or see my final days like I had done while under hypnosis. It was merely a flash. I don't know what it's like for someone else to have a vision from a prior life, but I know the difference because of the feeling or emotion that comes over me, and unless you have had this experience, it's very hard to explain.

Another extremely vivid vision that came to me was in a dream. It was as though the dream was in fact a reality. I drove past my husband's place of employment, which wasn't unusual for me, and came to a red traffic light just past his workplace. I sat at the light and looked over at a woman with blond hair driving a white van, and I remember thinking two things to myself. One, I didn't like her. Two, she had a really bad perm. The dream felt so real to me that when I woke up, I told my husband at the time about it and he didn't really say too much in that moment. Eventually, time passed and more was revealed to me. It turned out that the woman I saw in my dream was the woman he was having an affair with at his job in real life. I hadn't given it much thought at the time of the dream, but the work vehicles they all drove at his job were white. And he later admitted to me the accuracy of the "bad perm" I had seen during my dream. He admitted the inner shock he experienced when I was telling him about my dream because she had actually just gone to the salon and ended up walking out very unhappy due to the bad perm. I couldn't believe what I was hearing. Believe it or not, I was so excited. I was excited about having a premonition that had been so accurate.

For quite some time prior to this premonition, I had been realizing that I no longer wanted to be married. We got together at such a young age and I felt that the growth of my soul and who I was meant to be had been stunted. I had a lot of growing up to do. We both did. I was feeling like I needed to spread my wings and experience life, and staying married wasn't going to allow me to have the life experiences that my soul needed. When we had gotten together, I was sixteen and he was fifteen, and we started a family by the time I was eighteen years old. I simply couldn't stay, but he needed to be okay. I had mapped out exactly how I wanted and needed our relationship to end, had fantasized about how it was all going to happen with a close friend, and even wrote about it in my diary. The plan I had for him was that he needed to find someone else. He needed to feel that it was his decision in order to accept that it was over and allow me to open my wings to fly. I had played it over and over again in my head so much that I could literally feel the emotion of going through the separation. I had even worked out what I was going to say to him when I found out he had met another woman. When it all came to light, without placing any blame or being angry, I let him know that it was okay that he had found someone else. We were young when we first got together, so it was okay. And from that moment on, we discovered a great friendship.

During what could have been one of the darkest times in my life, I was having what felt like a rebirth, shedding one life chapter and getting ready to start anew. Instead of feeling the loss of my marriage and life that I knew for so long, I was starting to recognize that I had important gut feelings and I wasn't really alone. Odd, but this was how I felt. I later learned that when I had come to this crossroads and was being pointed in a certain direction, accompanied by feelings of contentment and even excitement for what was to come, this was my Spiritual Guide communicating to me through my gut instinct. I remember feeling comforted and happy instead of sad and depressed. This is usually a sign that you are on the right path!

Now that I have grown spiritually, working with Joann and Cindy, I look back at this now and see that I actually had manifested the outcome that I wanted. I now realize that what you put out into the Universe, it will in fact deliver.

It was also during this transition that I had a great "aha" moment. It was when I finally realized what I was looking for, the gift I was told I had so many years ago. It was literally staring back at me every day when I looked in the mirror. It was nothing unique to me at all, which was why I had such a hard time finding it! It wasn't anything different to me. It was normal and just a part of who I am. Here I had spent years looking for something unique. Something that stood out. It never occurred to me that maybe my normal was not exactly normal to anyone else. Once I had that realization I was able to look back at many "moments" that had happened that were "normal" for me but not necessarily "normal" for most. This gift I had was the gift of feeling and knowing. I am empathic.

I remember it as clear as day when it came to me. I was driving from a day of hiking, followed by visiting my uncle with a cousin, and somehow we got into a conversation on the drive home about paranormal and psychic stuff, and she had mentioned empaths and what that meant. It never occurred to me after all these years that there were different types of psychic abilities. Empath had clicked with me -- it totally defined what I had been looking for. You have no idea how relieved I felt to finally "define" what my gift was so I could now work on developing it.

This is how things would often work with me. While talking to a friend about someone they were most concerned about, the conversation would randomly become an emotional, uncanny and insightful bridge for me to the person they were speaking about. I always knew when it was happening because I would get a tingling sensation and the hairs on my arms would raise. Looking back on many different times when I thought I was giving friendly advice to my friends and family, I now know it was much more than that. The advice I gave came from another place. Here I was being "activated" and didn't know what that meant or what it was at the time. When I connected to their loved one, as I mentioned earlier, I had a very distinct sense of knowing with passion. The words would flow out of me, with intuitive feelings and emotions making me very passionate about what I'm advising. The advice I was delivering became my own personal reality and my truth. It was as though I had become their loved one. Still to this day my challenge is learning how to connect and disconnect from being "activated." I never know when or why sometimes I am able to connect, and once I'm connected, I can't disconnect.

When I started becoming more comfortable with this new understanding, I decided to give it a test. When I was in college, I was talking to a classmate and she was telling me about her eccentric uncle who had recently passed away. Her mom was looking for something specific that she knew he had left behind. Whether that was money, jewelry, letters, or something else, I had no clue. As she told me this story, out of the blue, it was as though I inherited the emotions, motivations, and feelings of her uncle. I prefaced what I was getting ready to tell her with, "this may sound odd to you but... your uncle told your mom where "it" is. Not directly but almost through subtle hints in one of his odd letters or notes he had written to her. There was something he wrote her that will clearly point out where this is "hidden" in his house.

It may be through a secret brother/sister code or language that only they would understand, but he somehow told her." This is where I received my first big validation! She went back and told her mom, it turned out I was right and she was able to find what she was looking for.

When I'm around my daughter, Joann, or Cindy I have these "feelings" of "tapping in." When this happens, I'll say that I am "activated" or simply say, "Just so you know, this is not coming from me" and then I share what's coming to me at that moment. When this happens, I am not given an opportunity to interject with my own opinions or thoughts, not even "on the inside," because messages come to me so rapidly that it feels as though it becomes my reality and my truth. This forces me to be very focused on delivering the message, uninterrupted, which is my challenge when I'm with Joann and Cindy. To know them is to know that if you aren't a communicative bull then you probably aren't going to be given an opportunity to say much, if anything at all. As I often say to Joann, and Cindy... "Just sayin." The exception is when I may find myself in a situation where a Spirit is angry. I've been known to turn into a "bitch" which is not typical of my personality, or so I am told. If I am with anyone other than my daughter, Joann, or Cindy, I normally will push these messages away because frankly I don't want to be judged.

Joann has often asked me why I think I may get messages and feel activated more so when I'm around her and Cindy. When I pondered this, I realized the reason is that when I am with Joann or Cindy, I don't have the fear of judgment. This allows me to just be open to who I am and to any and all messages I may receive. When you learn to tap into your intuition this way and to trust it, a whole world of insight opens up for you.

My mom was fearless and did not care about others judging her. I realize now that this was probably why her gifts came through in such a strong way. For example, I can recall close friends and family poking fun at my mom for her gifts. Although my mom was sought out by many for her gifted advice, I can recall many of those people, mostly family members, teasing her and calling her a witch. Boy, would this really set her coals on fire. My mom was NOT one you would want to piss off. She was a four-foot-ten redhead who took shit from NO one, regardless of who you were. She did not care where you came from, how big or small you were, male or female, or what your status in society. She treated everyone equally and if you pissed her off, she would only toss back whatever was thrown at her. One of the adjectives I remember used to describe here was "Spit Fire." But if she loved you, she would do anything for you. My mom didn't really care about being judged or not, she would just put "it" out there and if you didn't like it that was your problem, not hers. I am not like that. I'd rather just pick and choose who I trust and who I share this side of myself with.

It took me such a long time to unveil what my gift was that if I started sharing my intuition and messages with my old friends, they would probably just look at me like I had completely lost my marbles and think I was full of shit. I tend to think that some may already think I have a few screws loose anyway. I had one old friend who I had opened up to and shared this side of myself with, and I talked to her about different experiences I had had, but unfortunately she suddenly passed away. This totally ripped my heart out, and she was the girlfriend I had shared the Ouija experience with. Lately, as I make new friends, I am more apt to share this side of myself with them when I feel I can trust them or feel they aren't skeptics. I completely understand that "this world" isn't for everyone, and if you are of the mindset that you have to see it to believe it, then you will definitely think I'm a nut. A part of the reason I am more apt to tell new friends about this side of myself is mostly because I can hear Joann's voice in the back of my mind saying, "You need to embrace your gift."

Over time I have seen my ability change. I have found myself no longer needing someone to create a bridge for me to connect to someone else while having a conversation. The first time I met Cindy, I experienced a first. I met Cindy because Joann told me she had someone she wanted me to meet because she believed she and I had some similarities, and she may be someone I could talk to and share some of my experiences with. All I can say is thank God I was in the right company. I remember standing in Cindy's kitchen eating area with Joann and Cindy, feeling the presence and emotions of a female spirit. It was an older lady who was very sad. I could feel her emotions and felt them becoming a part of me. I started feeling overwhelmed by her sadness and I was having trouble holding back her tears. I started crying. I couldn't believe it. Here I had never met Cindy before, and I was standing in her house at my first introduction, crying with no valid reason other than connecting to a Spirit. The emotions were not mine; the tears did not belong to me. I was merely a vessel to display the emotions of this Spirit and share what she was feeling and thinking. Try explaining that to a skeptic! Had it been anyone else they would have given me a nice white jacket with extra-long sleeves and had called me a ride to be taken away to a new place to call home with padded walls. Unbelievable! Now was not the time for me to be experiencing a first like this. This was the first time I had an outward experience in front of anyone and was the first of more to come.

Another memorable experience was also at Cindy's house. Joann and I went to visit, and this time we all sat at her dining room table with Cindy sitting at the head of the table and Joann and I sat across from one another on either side of Cindy. I don't recall the conversation we were having, but what stands out in my mind was that every time I looked at Cindy I was getting a vision of her sobbing. I wasn't able to shake it. It was distracting me from being able to be present in the conversation. Finally, I gave in and had to tell her what I was seeing. As I opened up and shared what I was seeing, the more visions I started to get. Another first. What I shared with Cindy that day ended up being a premonition of a series of events that later came true for her.

Since then I have come to learn that my ability to pay attention to my Spiritual Guides has grown. I was reminded by Joann that my Spirit Guide is always with me, this is also something my mom used to tell me. I was so young when my mom told me this. I never realized until around the time I started working with Joann and Cindy that my gut instincts all this time were really coming from my Spirit Guide, who we call "Chief", talking to me and guiding me. This made me realize that this was why I did not feel alone when my ex-husband and I parted ways, as I'd mentioned before.

I have also met two other guides that "walk" with me spiritually. The one guide who is my Spirit Reiki Guide is a monk. He came to me through an opening meditation when I went for my Reiki certification. The entire experience was quite profound. There was an enormous amount of energy flow and exchange that day. I saw him, in my mind's eye, dressed in his monk attire, and he was welcoming and friendly as well as humorous. When I asked his name during the meditation, he chuckled and told me I wouldn't be able to pronounce it so just call him "Zed." Since then he stands by my side and helps guide me in Reiki sessions to direct the energy where it needs to go for my clients.

My other guide came to me at the end of 2017, early 2018. I've been told by Joann that she is a gypsy woman whose name is Clara. Since she has come, I noticed that

I've become more "activated", allowing me to have more insight into myself and others.

It's been a long journey for me. There were many times I felt that I'd never learn what the gifts were that I'd been told about that I needed to develop. But now I feel I'm on a really exciting Spiritual path that has only just begun.

PART II:
STORIES AND ADVENTURES

WILLIAMSBURG, VIRGINIA

As the three of us have been on this path, continuing our journey in the world of healing and of Spirit, we are grateful for many interesting experiences and adventures, a few of which we would like to share with you. Although each of us has our own unique gifts, we all have one common goal, which is healing the mind, body and soul of our many clients. The common threads we share are empathy, intuition, and a desire to help people. We have laughed and cried, and we have sometimes disagreed, but we always manage to stay connected. We work together on a physical level, but even more so on a spiritual level. We have come to learn that our souls have been connected in past lives and we will understand this concept more as we move forward and continue to grow. We have had many positive experiences, and some not so positive, but the journey is never boring!

We have had many opportunities to discover and work at sacred sites and places rich in history. We have been to Williamsburg, Princeton Battlefield, Jockey Hollow, Washington's Morristown Headquarters, Washington Rock, the mill and beautiful old homes of Allentown, N.J., Perth Amboy, Clinton, and various other historic districts in New Jersey and Pennsylvania. We have helped people to rid their homes of unwanted energies and we have conducted many paranormal investigations. We have found spirit activity outdoors in the beautiful cranberry bogs of Whitesbog, NJ and on the beaches of Sandy Hook. We have found Spirit activity indoors in Thomas Edison's famous laboratory and at Doris Duke's estate. We have spent time in famous and not so famous cemeteries, and in many former brothels. Our paranormal investigations produce EVP recordings from many of these places, oftentimes with messages that served to confirm exactly what we picked up along the way.

Psychic Treasures Unlimited took an extended trip to Williamsburg that was amusing at times, difficult at times, and which taught us so much about Spirit and the respect we must always have for all souls. We all knew from the very moment we set foot on the streets of historic Williamsburg that the place was full of history and also full of Spirits.

We never take an extended trip without some chaos. This time, we came close to losing Aleja in the bowels of Washington, DC when she almost ran out of gas. After some nail biting, she finally arrived in Williamsburg and we lost no time starting our adventure.

We decided to step out that first evening well after dark as it was fairly quiet and uncrowded, which made it much easier for us to connect to Spirit and to use our equipment. We were there at a time of year when the crowds were relatively thin. We parked in a dark and empty parking lot that immediately set the tone, and we set off toward the stark and empty Capitol building at the very end of town. We were walking down a wide dirt road with old houses to the left and right, as we approached the big brick Capitol building that was gated across the front. We noticed a couple of other brave souls, two teenage girls who came around the corner and were goofing around in front of the large gated entrance. Joann, who was on full alert, suddenly said, "There is a Spirit hanging around those girls over by the front gate. He is communicating with me. Aleja, Cindy, look closely now and watch what that Spirit is about to do to those two girls! He is shaking the bars of the gate as they are approaching!" We watched intently, and as the girls came closer to the building they were laughing loudly and joking around about all those "badass Spirits" in Williamsburg. They were completely clueless that there was a Spirit right in front of them. Suddenly one of them screamed in terror, "Oh my God, what WAS that?" The other one, equally panic-stricken, yelled, "I don't know, but get me OUT OF HERE!" These girls started running for their lives, as if they HAD seen a ghost. Joann chuckled, saying that the Spirit had put his hand through the bar of the gate and touched them, deliberately attempting to strike fear into them. We knew in that moment we were going to have an interesting few days ahead of us.

We approached the gate once the girls were out of sight, and Joann asked the Spirit "Why did you do that?" He replied, "Because I can and because it is amusing." He then said, "People stare at us all day like we are a circus act. Sometimes it's funny to make them afraid. You tourists are very annoying to us." He made us think, and we told him that we had nothing but respect for the Spirits.

We ventured around the town until almost midnight. We were doing so much exploring and probing deeper and deeper into the world of Spirit that was here. Historic Williamsburg, recreated to look exactly as it did a few hundred years ago, seems firmly stuck in the past along with all the Spirits that inhabit it. We wondered if this is why so many Spirits remain there.

Eventually we made small talk with a nice security guard and asked about the Spirit activity in town. "Oh, EVERY person who works security here will tell you there are all kinds of crazy things happening all the time. I would say that if you spend any extended amount of time here, you cannot help but believe that Spirits do exist. They make our lives crazy every day."

We were fascinated and wanted to explore more, and we asked if it would be ok for us to use our paranormal equipment around Colonial Williamsburg late at night. This is when the area is relatively vacant and the Spirits seem very active. The security guard said it was fine, but to keep it on the down low. We set up our paranormal equipment based on where Joann was seeing activity. Joann is our eyes and ears, a completely open portal to Spirit, always pointing us in the right direction.

Although our equipment was receiving constantly to

let us know that there was indeed Spirit activity, our batteries were being immediately drained by all this Spirit energy around us. We have found this battery drain to be a common occurrence when there are many Spirits gathered in one place. We could not obtain any recordings.

As the evening wore on and Joann was picking all kinds of information up, the Spirits were becoming more and more agitated. Our intuition let us know that we were imposing on the privacy of these souls and that they were angry and frustrated, yet we still continued. It was almost like we were poking and bothering them during the wee hours of the night when all they wanted was to finally be left alone. We realized that in this historic place, with all the big crowds, these Spirits never get a break. They don't have any peace. They are always under a microscope being observed.

We met another security guard at the Bruton Episcopal Church, which had pews that had once been reserved for George Washington, Thomas Jefferson, and many other important early leaders of this nation. He informed us that virtually every single night alarms go off in the church. Cindy asked if there is ever a time when Spirit activity is most active, and he replied without hesitation, "Oh yes, things get really crazy here during the full moon. We always prep ourselves around that time, knowing that it will be busier than normal. Every so often a sprinkler system will go off without real cause. Security alarms go off everywhere, and we have to check out every incident to make sure each place is safe. Most of the time during a full moon we cannot figure out what the heck set the alarm off. More often than not, there is no logical explanation or sign of people around." He remembered the story of one especially crazy night when the church alarms were going off, they went into the building. They saw books being thrown across the room, but there was no living person there. He looked frightened telling the story, as if it was an image he did not love to recall, and an incident he did not want to repeat. "Ok, you three have a nice evening. Y'all are crazy to seek after these Spirits here. Let 'em be." In hindsight, it might have been better if we had taken heed of his advice.

The next day we returned to the churchyard, and we could all feel so much energy in the cemetery just outside the building. Joann was communicating with Spirit and so many souls had things to say! We had a new sense of respect after hearing the guards' stories from the night before, and we were all extremely careful not to step on the gravestones. At one point, Joann stepped on one poor innocent soul by accident and quickly stated, "No disrespect. I'm so sorry." Cindy looked at Joann like she was losing her mind. At times along this journey, we forget which world we are living in, on earth or in the world of Spirit. Sometimes the lines get blurred.

The following night we decided to check out a ghost tour. We are usually the ones presenting the ghost tours, so we thought it would be kind of cool to actually be guests in the audience this time. Throughout the tour, Joann kept saying, "These Spirits do not appreciate these tours going on every night, invading every aspect of the lives they led and uncovering all their past secrets. I am really just overwhelmed with the feeling that they want to be left alone." Cindy and Aleja were both feeling this too, a general sense of uneasiness that we were doing something wrong. The tour eventually took us to the Peyton Randolph house, considered one of the most haunted buildings in America. Cindy recalled the night before when security had mentioned this place as one of the buildings where alarms were constantly being tripped with no logical explanation.

As the tour group collected in front of this famous historic home, Joann distinctly heard a male Spirit yelling out angrily, "Leave! You are not welcome!" Joann stated this observation out loud to the people around us, and the next moment security pulled up to enter the house because the alarms started going off. The tour guide looked at the three of us in our Psychic Treasures Unlimited shirts and figured he might as well let us take over the tour. He might have been onto something.

At this point, the tour guide suggested we all take some pictures of the Peyton Randolph house because he said the Spirits have been known to regularly show up in random photos, especially at this location. Next thing you know, Joann is telling everyone exactly where to focus their cameras based upon where she was seeing Spirits in the house. Joann was really focused on a certain window upstairs where she could see and feel activity. She snapped a photo of this window, and everyone else on the tour did too.

We all started excitedly comparing photos, and low and behold, the only photo with two distinct Spirits showing up in that one window came from Joann's phone. This photo was amazing! To this day, it is one of the best photos of Spirit that we have ever obtained, and we have many. Cindy was busy taking down everyone's phone numbers on the tour. They wanted us to share the photo with them because this was the only photo taken that night that actually revealed two spirits in the window.

On our final night in Williamsburg we were checking out a large courtyard area that had houses all around the perimeter. Back in the day this area had served as the town green where a lot of social activity and gatherings occurred. It was so surreal because the Spirits started to come out and gather around us while we were standing there. Joann stated, "This is starting to feel like a party, and we are the main event, if you know what I mean."

"Yes," replied Cindy, "I am feeling crowded and suffocated." When there are many Spirits present, Cindy tends to get constriction in her chest like she cannot breathe, and she feels very heavy. She can feel spirit touch and sense their emotions. Joann tends to get headaches, and Aleja gets the sensation of having goosebumps that are not visible, and the hair stands up on the back of her neck. Aleja's mind's eye opens and she can see. It happens all at once and then she is able to see what is there. She describes it as a completely separate vision, like she is seeing with a separate set of eyes. This situation is usually accompanied by emotion which, in this particular case, was fear because these Spirits were not being friendly. "I feel like we are being invaded, and it's not a good feeling," Aleja confirmed.

Suddenly, while we were standing there assessing what the heck was going on, Joann looked over at a large building at the end of the green and said, "Cindy! Aleja! I see a young male Spirit frantically jumping back and forth over the tall wall in front of that building. He is really freaking out! He wants us to help find his girlfriend!" Cindy picked up her phone and started to research the history of this particular building. Joann lovingly refers to Cindy as "Lois Lane" because she usually hops right on the research to figure out what Joann might be picking up. Cindy was shocked and started to tell the story to Aleja and Joann. She said, "Apparently, this is an exact replica of a building that served on these grounds as an insane asylum for a few hundred years. It was first established in 1773 as The Publick Hospital for Persons of Insane and Disordered Minds and later became known as The Eastern Lunatic Asylum. There was a murder that occurred right by the wall where Joann saw the Spirit jumping. Apparently for the college students at nearby William and Mary College, this was a favorite place for lovers to go. They would climb over the wall to get some privacy on the large rolling greens just inside the walls of the asylum. But one fateful night two lovers climbed the wall and the girl was met with the knife of a lunatic who had escaped his room in the asylum and was just waiting there to pounce and murder someone. The boy had pushed her over the wall first, and by the time he got over the wall and landed next to her, he found her bleeding to death." This story made so much sense to all of us because Joann kept saying that all the Spirits in that area were jumping around erratically, yelling and rocking back and forth. The young man jumping over the wall also seemed to be desperately searching for something.

The next thing we knew, we found ourselves standing in front of the George Wythe house on the town green. This house, although not as well-known as many of the other historic buildings in Williamsburg, to us seemed to have the darkest energy and the darkest Spirits we had encountered so far. Joann started to get very uncomfortable and warned, "That is one nasty Spirit inside that house, and he just instructed us to get in the car and leave." We were all feeling nervous and we decided that was a great idea, so we hopped in our car. Aleja was completely startled when she closed the car door, looked out the car window, and saw a Spirit pinned against the window staring back at her. Joann yelled out in a panic, "Guys, we are being surrounded! They are completely surrounding the car!" Cindy was in the backseat and could feel them touching her back, almost trying to pull her out of the car, and messing with her hair. "We need to get the hell out of here!" Aleja said firmly. She later recounted that she was receiving an intuitive message from these Spirits in which they were telling her if you are going to hunt for us, then we are going to turn around and haunt you. Aleja knew that we needed to get out of there quickly. She always takes the reins when things get tense, and she remains calm and logical under stress. If it weren't for Aleja, we might not still be here today in one piece! We left the scene quickly and were followed by Spirit for a while. None of us felt right the rest of that night or much of the next day. We had been taught a valuable lesson.

This event was one of the most frightening things that has happened to the three of us in all of our experiences with PTU. We learned from this trip that souls appear to have a difficult time healing and moving forward on their path when they are held under a microscope. Their heartache, their personal stories, their lessons and their karma are things they do not want on display! Spirits are unable to rest when they have people constantly studying them and the lives they led. Learning the basic history of an historic place is one thing, but each individual's skeletons in the closet (no pun intended!) should not be dragged out and mulled over for everyone in the modern day to observe. Whether alive or in Spirit, no soul wants that type of invasion of privacy. We are very grateful to have all learned this important lesson and to have all returned from this experience in one piece!

PENNINGTON, NEW JERSEY

For our next PTU adventure, we pulled up to a beautiful home in Pennington, New Jersey on a hot summer night when the mist hung heavy in the air. It seemed like the perfect evening, filled with mystery, in which to connect with Spirit. Someone had bid on "A Night out with Psychic Treasures Unlimited" at a school fundraising event and they won the bid to have us come do a paranormal and psychic investigation of their home. We were walking up the driveway and not even inside the home when Joann stopped thoughtfully and announced, "There's a male Spirit standing right here greeting us. His name is John and he is missing a leg." A typical dinner party night out with Psychic Treasures Unlimited.

The homeowner was standing there on the slate patio, ready to make introductions, and she replied in surprise, "Oh, I think I know who that is, that sounds like my grandfather, John. He did lose his leg in warfare." We made our introductions with a group that seemed somewhat skeptical at first glance. Aleja noted later, "Those homeowners seemed very cautious. They had a mindset like they were having some entertainment by letting these flakes walk through the house." Cindy felt they were humoring us about what we do, and they had a wall up around them. We said our prayer of protection and outlined our expectations for the evening's event in this lovely home.

We made our way inside the home and we all immediately felt a great deal of Spirit activity in a cozy room filled with books. Aleja recounted later that she kept it to herself that she was having trouble breathing in this room. Aleja tends to be quieter, whereas Cindy and Joann make up for her with their big mouths. Aleja often jokes that she can't get a word in edgewise when she is with the two of them.

There were four couples (in physical bodies) there that evening. Two of the men were very skeptical and seemed to consider this nothing more than amusing entertainment. Joann has a way of making people like that end up with their mouths hanging open by the time she is finished.

People are often skeptical about the possibility that others do have the ability to connect to Spirit. It's a skill that very few possess, and when people see something they cannot access and do not understand, they are often quick to dismiss it as impossible. This is sometimes fear-based. We often fear things for which there is no good explanation. What we do is not medical, it is not scientific, and it is often difficult to prove. But when you have good validation and offer things that could never be researched, like Joann does so very often, people do usually come around. Joann always feels good when she is helping Spirit to relay messages to their loved ones.

Spirit is very grateful as well because love never dies, and they want to let their loved ones know that they still exist, although in a different dimension that is nonphysical. Joann is not a nurse or a doctor, but she does heal in her own important way, through her ability to solidly connect the living with their loved ones who have crossed over. Your loved ones who have crossed over continue to see and hear everything that is going on in your life. They know your children, and your children's children, they attend holidays, birthdays and big life events. Do not ever think that your loved ones are missing something and you "wish they were here." They are!

At this point in the tour, we walked upstairs and turned left into a bedroom. Aleja was one of the first into this room. The guests filed in afterward, waiting on the edge of their seat to hear what we picked up about this room. None of us could breathe very well in here and we all felt inexplicably sad. Then Aleja just lost it. She said later that the most gut-wrenching, horrible, overwhelming sadness came over her and she started to cry. She explained to us that after this event in the bedroom she pretty much shut down for the rest of the investigation. She was embarrassed because she did not know these people, she was in their home having what looked like a breakdown, and after this occurred she just wanted to go home.

Joann explained that there had been a fire here and there was a woman who lost her child in the fire. Aleja was picking up the emotions of this woman. It all made sense to Aleja because she felt she was stuck and searching and felt the emotions of someone who did not want to leave until she found what she was looking for. Even after we left the room, Aleja remembers still feeling overwhelming horrific sadness. This intense emotion shut Aleja down, and she doesn't remember much else from the rest of the evening. The homeowners were shocked at this whole episode in the bedroom because they had access to the history of the home that they had not shared with us, and there had indeed been a well-documented fire that had destroyed parts of the home in that area of the house. The homeowners had deliberately shared no information with us, and they were quite surprised to find that they didn't need to. We were going to figure it out. Aleja was very grateful for the validation after her public display of emotion, and she was grateful to be trusted to open up and reveal her gifts that evening. She learned from this evening to really trust her gut and her emotions when she opens up in this way.

After this, we went into another bedroom upstairs with a story that turned out to be equally dramatic. Here Joann was seeing the spirit of a small child who was soaking wet. She was describing what this child looked like and what they were saying. At the same time, Steve and Cindy were in the basement with all the paranormal equipment on, picking up voice recordings of Spirit speaking. The amazing thing about this part of the night was that when Joann was describing and talking to the young child in the upstairs bedroom, the equipment was picking up the child's voice and the conversation down in the basement. As we often tell our clients, there is no geography on the other side. Spirit can connect across all time and space. The paranormal findings so often serve as validation for whatever has been picked up.

The hostess who owned the home suddenly lit up as if the notion had just hit her. Oh my, that young child you were speaking to is a family friend who passed. They drowned in a pool at their home a few years ago. Our children used to play together.

If you remember, when we had arrived at this home earlier in the night, pointing out apparitions and doing some rituals to protect ourselves that probably seemed pretty out there, the guests at the party were amused and entertained, but definitely not taking us seriously. It was more like they felt that they had come to see the circus. By the time Psychic Treasures Unlimited left the home late that evening, these guests had each been given messages from their loved ones who had crossed, and also advice regarding their future direction. By the time the evening was over, the walls had come down for these people who mainly had labeled themselves non-believers when we had arrived. They were satisfied and happy and even somewhat excited over the findings and what was shared with them that night. They were definitely believers and convinced that we have real ability, and that this is not a joke. At the end of the evening, one of the hosts said that they had deliberately held back much information from us to see what would be picked up without any former knowledge. She said they really wanted to test us. We passed the test and more. This happens so often, where we walk into a group of skeptics and leave a group of believers. Open your mind, and you never know what you might learn.

A SMALL, QUAINT TOWN IN NEW JERSEY

Just a typical afternoon out with Joann, Cindy and Aleja in a quaint little historical town nestled somewhere in New Jersey. As we were wandering around, we came across a large hotel built in the 1800's and decided to go inside. Before even entering, Joann turned to Cindy and Aleja describing spirit activity of horses tied up to hitching posts out front along the street. As we entered the building, our curiosity was piqued, and we decided to seek out the manager to see if we could do some exploring inside. We explained to him who we were and why we were there. He then told us that other psychic mediums had explored the place at various times. He seemed a bit hesitant and did not provide us with any information, but he did decide to allow us to wander around. It was perfect timing for us because the place was mostly empty. There was a staircase nearby and so we decided to go up. When we got to the top of the stairs, we found we were most drawn to a room to the right. Upon entering the room, it was dark, and we all agreed that it had a creepy feel to it. It was only after a few short moments we all began to feel dizzy and nauseous. In the bathroom it seemed like there was an energetic footprint of a struggle or fight that had happened in this room. As we came out of the bathroom into a larger area where we were having conversation about what we were experiencing, individually, suddenly a door slammed. The place was completely still, not a window open or breeze present, and no explanation for this. We hightailed it out of that room!

We walked into the next room where it became very clear to Joann that a murder had once occurred. After walking in and out of a few other rooms, we then took the stairs down a level and entered into a room where Joann connected with a female Spirit. She told Joann that she had run a brothel in this hotel. She said this room had been her office because it was situated just below the "anything goes" room, which was the room just above. We realized that this was the dark, creepy room where we had sensed just moments ago an energetic footprint of a struggle or fight. The female Spirit shared that the male clients paid more to have extended time to do as they chose with their selected lady of the night.

As we returned back downstairs, Joann was getting a sense of many men dressed in military uniform with many ladies of the night accompanying them in the bar area.

The manager met with us before we left and we discussed our findings with him. He confirmed that the hotel had been a brothel and there had been a murder in the one room we mentioned.

OUR SPIRITUAL BOND

If there is one thing that we have learned through our experiences together, it is that we are connected spiritually. The connection we have to one another is best compared to that of a mother's connection to a child, giving her the gut instinct to know when she is needed. Some may think is it coincidence, or is it in fact a soul connection?

Joann has found throughout the years that her energy always seems to attract people, whether she is reading a client or just hanging out with friends. She often wonders, "Is it me, Joann, or is it my ability that makes these people want to be in my space? Could it be as simple as a past life soul connection?"

Working so closely with Cindy and Aleja, Joann has come to realize that there are important common threads between all of us, which are empathy, the fact that all of our abilities heighten when we are together, and past life soul connections. Most of all there is a strong bond of friendship. We all want to protect and help one another much like a parent helps their child. We all seem to tap into each other to either deliver a message, give advice or simply just listen when one of us needs it the most! It doesn't matter what time of day or night!

All three of us sense Spirit much more at nighttime when we have finally come to the end of our day and our minds have quieted down. When this happens to Cindy, Joann will often unexpectedly reach out or send a text to Cindy at the exact moment when she is sensing spirit activity. Joann has an uncanny ability to pick up on whatever Cindy is experiencing and tune into Cindy's environment right when an explanation is needed.

There are also so many times when Cindy and Joann are texting each other the same information at the same time. These types of connections have happened when Cindy was on vacation in the mountains, attending a college reunion, and at an event in New York City. Geography does not matter. This connection occurs no matter where we are.

Aleja recalls that on January 4, 2018, in the middle of the night, for whatever reason she woke up at 3:21 a.m. The reason she remembers the exact time is because she journaled about it. Aleja remembers waking up reaching for her phone (which she kept on "do not disturb") to see that Joann had been texting her at that exact moment. Joann was messaging her telling her she had picked up on a message from her Spirit Guide, Clara. Joann then asked Aleja, "Who is George?"

Aleja told her that George was who she recently bought her vehicle from. Joann gave her many messages that night, going from one subject to the next. Aleja remembers one specific message about someone very close to her, and believe it or not, that prediction came to fruition in 2019! Was it a coincidence that Aleja reached for her phone in the middle of the night right when these important messages were being delivered or was it a soul connection?

We have all come to be so grateful for our abilities and appreciate the support we all have for each other. In this lifetime, the three of us consider the bonds we share to be a soul connection.

PART III:
A WORD FROM OUR CLIENTS

Psychic Treasures Unlimited has not just been built by Joann, Cindy and Aleja, but also by our clients. After all these years we want them all to know how important each and every one of them have been to each of us individually.

There were far too many stories, shared by our clients to print but we are grateful to have received them all and hope that you will enjoy reading a few stories told in their words instead of ours.

JOANN

We were in a crowded café, listening to tango music. I glanced across the table at him and I reached out my index finger to touch his. He smiled and asked what I was doing and I whispered, "We're connected." Little did I realize how telling these words would be – I felt it. I knew. And when he left, I felt an immense fear. I was floating lost. I wondered, "Is the cord severed now?"

I remembered years prior, after my mother passed, I went to see someone who told me about Joann. She said, "She's really good." I wasn't ready. But this was different. I lost my husband, my soulmate. I knew I had to at least try. Not everyone would choose to see a medium after their loved one passes, but I needed answers. Is there truly life after life? Are we still connected as I originally believed? Does life spiral outward? When I arrived for my session, I was anxious. I didn't know he would do as I secretly asked and come with me. Joann helped me to see that we are still connected and always will be.

When I sat down for my first reading, she told me she would be direct – another sign. Having lived in Germany, it is the way – be direct. When she started talking about the presence of a male spirit who couldn't catch his breath, I knew it was him. She went on to tell me details about my husband and our life. When she delivered his messages, I knew that he was indeed there. His message was in part to "get a grip" as love never dies.

I have been to see Joann a second time and she has renewed my faith in life after this life. We do indeed go on. I know it, like I knew when I touched my finger next to his, that my husband and I are and always will be – connected. Joann put me at ease. Her approach is genuine and demonstrates her ability with grace, I so appreciate that. Two worlds connected. I have witnessed it. I have partaken in the process and I have been gifted a way forward.
-S.K.

———————————————

About 8 to 10 years ago, I remember calling to schedule a date for a psychic party at my house. Joann worked with the psychic I had requested, and when I called, Joann answered the phone and started to go over all details of having this party. She also promoted her services as a medium. At the time, I didn't know much about them. The only medium that I heard about was the one on TV, John Edwards, the man who talked to "dead people." Fascinated by this subject, I began asking her questions like "How did you know you were a medium?" "How old were you?" "Can you also come to the psychic party?" In her responses she actually began to give me a free reading. She asked me if my mom had passed away. She also asked me if she was Italian and spoke with an Italian accent. Mind you if my name showed up on her caller ID, there would be no indication that I was of Italian descent. My first name is Spanish and last name Hungarian.

"Yes, yes," I replied. Then she said to me that my mother came to her and she wants to tell me "zabaglione." Zabaglione? I'm thinking the word sounds familiar but forgot what it meant in Italian. She said that it might not make sense to you now, but it will later on. Next, she told me that she can see two men playing cards and one of them said something to her and the way he said it made her laugh. She said that she wants to repeat it exactly the way he said it (with his accent) "I hate American food!!" She asked me if I knew who that could be. I almost dropped the phone. The man was my brother-in-law. He hated American food and would repeat it constantly. He would not allow his sister who came to visit him from Italy to eat any fast foods or any processed food, especially brown gravy made from an envelope. Joann continued to tell me more, but those two significant statements will remain in my memory forever because the next day my mother's message to me came to light. The next day I told my coworkers about the crazy experience I had with Joann, the medium. When I mentioned the confusing message of "zabaglione" from my mom, my girlfriend immediately recognized the word and made the connection. She reminded me that a week prior she and I were in class teaching our students about different traditions and cultures around the world. For an example, I told them that my mom was born and raised in Italy and when I was about 10 years old, my mom would make me a drink made with two raw eggs beaten, sugar, and a touch of Marsala wine for breakfast. I'd drink it every morning before school. I had forgotten the name of that drink and asked if anyone of my students were Italian and if so, to please ask their family what this recipe was called. Well, apparently my mom must have been in my classroom that day because she responded with – zabaglione. Remarkable!! You just can't make this up!!

-C.L.

The first time I had a session with Joann I sat down across from her taking notes. She asked me about a gentleman who had passed. She told me that he loved me. I took a picture out and showed it to her, because I wasn't sure if this was the gentleman she was speaking about. Turned out that it was. All of a sudden, we started hearing music. Joann looked out the window to see if someone was outside since we were the only people in the house. As she kept talking, the music got louder and louder. She got up and went into the hall and saw that the TV was on. It had not been on when I arrived. On the television, Andrea Bocelli was singing. He is one of my favorite singers and is very much associated with the gentleman who had passed. We had seen him in concert together. I had just been asking Joann if this person still loved me. The song was in Italian and it was a love song. Joann told me that something like this had never happened to her before, and we both got goosebumps at the same time! We could see that not only were we the only ones in the house, but the TV remote was across the room and not even facing the TV. Joann assured me it was a definite sign from my loved one. This so touched my heart I will always remember this experience.

-S.E.

———————————————

Joann's first reading with me was spot on. There was no mistaking she was communicating with my father on the other side. She stated my name three times while banging her hand on the desk. This was clearly something my dad would have done if I was not listening to him when he was alive. She mentioned things that only my dad would know. She described my driving details, like how I put my purse on my lap while driving to search for something. Not a good idea! When communicating with my dad, Joann told me that when I see a red cardinal it is a sign that my dad is around. One day as I was driving and speaking to my dad, I asked him to let me know if I was doing the right thing. I looked to my right and smiled. There was a "red cardinal" truck that drove right past me, and the driver honked!! Ask and you shall receive.

Joann has also told me various things that would happen, including a new job offer in around 7-8 weeks, even what type of job—it happened! She also predicted relationship issues that she said would happen with those

I am close to, and yes, they all happened! I have noticed that Joann sometimes brings up some of the same things in several readings. When I remind her that she said the same thing last time, she simply says she does not remember one reading to the next. She confirms that if she repeats something to me several times then it's going to happen, so pay attention. Guess what? A week or two later, the prediction that she had repeated over several readings did come to light.

-K.G.

I met the ladies of Psychic Treasures Unlimited several years ago when they would host an annual "Witches Night Out" event in my local town. It was an awesome event where the ladies would take groups of people on a "ghost walk" around town. After my first reading with Joann I was hooked. I even had my mom and grandmother travel from Pittsburgh, PA to get a reading from Joann. In that reading, she connected with my Uncle Dave, my grandmother's son. He had passed the year before from lung cancer. He was a young-hearted, vibrant, Harley-riding, sweet guy. It is absolutely without a doubt in my mind that Joann had connected with him. Even her mannerisms changed to be like his and the things that she would say sounded exactly like him, the words she chose and her body language. She totally brought comfort to my grandmother who was still very much mourning the loss of her first born. But the story gets better...

I try to set up a reading with Joann every 6 months or so, just to check in/tune in and get validation that I'm on the right path. During one of my regular "check-up" appointments, Joann immediately picked up on the fact that my mom was not feeling well, which was correct. My mom had been diagnosed with Non-Hodgkins Lymphoma. After that struggle, she had been cancer free for the past 2 1/2 years. During one of her recent checkups, however, the doctors realized that something was wrong, and they were running many tests. As we were waiting for the results I went for my reading with Joann. Joann did not know any of this was going on. But she immediately picked up on the fact that my mom was not doing so well, and she told me that it was lung cancer and it was going to progress very quickly. I was devastated. How could she know this? Should I even believe her? Joann is straight to the point. She doesn't sugar coat. She tells you exactly what you need to know. My uncle came through and told her that he would be there when my mom crossed over. Joann said that my mom would be going to the hospital, but there would be no treatment this time. She encouraged me to spend as much time as I could with her and make sure that she got to see my kids and to take her on a trip. My reading with Joann was on a Tuesday. That Thursday, 2 days later, my mom was in the hospital. The doctors met with us and told us that the prognosis was not good. On top of the cancer being back, my mom also had pneumonia. Treatments were not an option as she would not survive them. They told us to start preparing for her final arrangements. I heard everything Joann told me play over and over again in my head. As my mom was released from the hospital, I made sure she visited with my kids and we even took a short trip that I was very grateful for. After my mom passed, I went to see Joann to have another "check-up." She was able to connect with my mom and validate so many things I still needed to hear. It brings me so much comfort to know that my mom is still with me.

L.M.

I scheduled my reading with Joann because I had recently lost my father unexpectedly. It was not a natural decision for me to make as I have always tended to be a bit of a skeptic. However, after a few "strange coincidences" after my father's death and a gentle push, I decided to go and see what would happen. I figured I had nothing to lose and everything to gain.

I had a very successful reading if one measures success by the number of spirits who came through during my session. I am the de facto historian/genealogist of my family, so I brought many pictures and stories for Joann. Almost everyone to whom I wanted to try and connect came through, including my dad. I had some burning questions answered, learned some unknown facts and had some exasperated spirit guides advise me about my ongoing history of being extremely accident-prone!

My story didn't end there, however. As my session was wrapping up and we were just basically chatting about nothing of consequence, Joann scribbled something on a piece of paper and said she wanted to tell me something else. She told me that she had recently begun to be able to tap into some people's past lives. There was no rhyme or reason as to whom she could do this with, and she also said she didn't understand why she was beginning to have this skill or what it meant for her at the time. With that said, she looked at me and told me I had been brutally murdered in a past life. I just looked at her and said with almost relief, "I KNOW IT - I KNEW IT!!!!"

It was as if a lightbulb had been turned on and a lot of things instantly made sense. I offered her some details that I suspected had happened to me in that life, and she confirmed most of them. I have spent a good part of my adult life being plagued by a particular recurring, horrific and brutal nightmare - always taking place in the same setting with the same ending. I always wrote this nightmare off as a result of some kind of stress I was under at the time of the nightmare - everyone always has their own "stress" dream/nightmare.

Joann and I were able to piece together some details, including a back story with some context and a possible time period for my murder - it feels strange putting that in writing. She felt that this had been one of my most important past lives, and one that would make an imprint on my life now. Surprisingly, instead of freaking me out, this revelation actually gave me peace of mind. I've had my "nightmare" one or two times since my reading, but it has been less intense and terrifying. Maybe it's less of a mystery now so I feel more in control when I am experiencing it.

I went into my reading very skeptical and doubting whether or not I would have any kind of experience. I came out of my appointment feeling very strong, empowered and supported.
-S.H.

My daughter is a client of Joann's and has shared many of Joann's readings with me. She has explained how Joann taught her about Spirit. Specifically, my daughter related Joann's understanding of how the afterlife works and the things that Joann claims are signs from Spirit.

I was diagnosed with cancer very suddenly and it brought me to be hospitalized. During this time, I had a near death experience. I can only begin to explain it as I was somewhere...in sort of a void...but suddenly shown right in front of me was a slideshow of my life. It was my life from the moment I was born until the present day, all the pertinent and even mundane, but spiritually relevant, events of my time on earth in this body. It was being shown to me as pages of a book, very quickly. Some memories I remembered, and some I hadn't. I was seeing all my steps of life, both good and bad, for the last 60 years.

But meanwhile, back on the hospital table, I was later told that I had flat lined. I suspect that this was the same moment I was presented my slideshow. All I knew was that I was no longer in my body, but what happened next made me question how that could be...

I felt I was in Grand Central Station! Yes, you heard that right. The slideshow ended and now I felt myself standing at what appeared to be a ticket window, yet no attendant nor sign, just a counter. On the other side of this counter, I could see the vast, breathtaking architecture like Grand Central. People were busy coming and going, focused on their own agendas. To my right was floor to ceiling bookshelves of files that went on for what seemed like miles.

Somehow, I knew that the people saw me behind the counter but would only acknowledge me like a visitor taking a brief glimpse. Then I happened to look down and I saw a stack of folders. Each folder was labeled with a name. As I went through each one, I recognized all the names of my friends and family who had passed from cancer. In fact, I recognized one of the people I had known in life walk past me in the station, too. She had died when she was a young girl, but seemed to be around

30 years old here, and very healthy.

Oddly, I was not shown a folder for my mom who had passed the year before of lung cancer. Deep down, I somehow knew her folder was absent by design. A folder for my mom would remind me that she was there and how terribly I missed her. She did not want to give me reason to stay. And, I had already seen her in a separate vision and she had told me that I needed to get better. It was not my time - my husband and children needed me on earth.

With constant CPR and paddling going on in my hospital bed, as I was later told, I found myself suddenly leaving the station and back on a table in the hospital. I no longer possessed the peaceful and pain- free feeling that I had just experienced on the other side. And I was still unconscious, but alive. I later recall, while on life support, remembering my mom as she was shaking her finger at me cautioning, "You better get better! Do you hear me?!"

During the rest of my time sitting in that hospital room day after day throughout recovery, I felt others in there with me, like angels keeping watch. In fact, right after this near-death experience, a saline drip bag, which we all know hangs by being wrapped around the coiled end of a pole, managed to unhook itself and get thrown on the floor in front of my husband and daughters. Visitors perhaps?

While sharing this story with my daughter a week later, she told me that Joann had told her about this Book of Life, where your Spirit Guide shows you your life in full, before you cross over to the other side. It then gets stored in a library. This is exactly what I had seen! Joann also had told my daughter that when our loved ones come through to her in Spirit, they always look their best. Joann's descriptions gave validation to what I had just seen in my own experience, and I now firmly believe in this woman's ability to connect to the other side. Even more, I realize that there IS something much bigger than ourselves; that each of us and our soul has an important task to complete while we are here.

-V.H.

CINDY

I had the opportunity to meet with Cindy for a Meditation/Manifestation session. After many years of battling depression and OCD (obsessive-compulsive disorder) I had accumulated paper clutter. For someone that has OCD it was difficult to let go of and felt very overwhelming to me at times. I think she was surprised by my request since most people look for love, money, weight loss, etc. I just wanted Cindy to "get rid of my stuff!" We both laughed about it – which really helped! We then discussed how Meditation/Manifestation could assist with this issue. She was very comforting and gave me various tools to use in my healing process. Her message was clear that everyone has something that they are dealing with and you can apply these skills to anything. Anytime that I have a question I speak to Cindy, knowing her guidance will assist me.

Her many meditation audio recordings have brought me comfort and I continue to use them along with her other techniques for my daily life challenges.
-D.L.

Cindy stood on my doorstep on a bright summer day

with an adorable smile and clip holding back a whisk of hair, ready to help me embrace a "whole lot of spiritual and calming potential"; undoubtedly, she was completely snowed by the difficult client in front of her. I remember thinking how this girl was in for a MEGA challenge! - I needed to sell my house, find a new job, find a new place to live and quell my anxiety attacks in newfound singlehood, so that my kids still knew Mom was "OK" and not certifiable.

Cindy sat in my living room like a lifelong friend-engaged, real, and hell-bent on figuring out where the Universe and I stood; and to set my butt straight, no matter how difficult, with such an anxiety-laden body.

Cindy managed to teach me that day, as well as the days ahead, that the power of the mind and the soul is a power unlike anything you can fathom. If you can connect them to speak the same language, you can unlock wonderful ways to help you finally breathe. And for me, forget "shine", I just wanted to breathe. With her soothing voice, she instructed me to breathe and relax. She said, "Concentrate on emptying your thoughts away from your daily stresses, quiet and empty your mind." This was so beneficial to me, if even for a few minutes. She gave me tools to stay in the present moment which she told me was so important for my mental health and well-being. If you release your focus from the stresses of the past or the worries of the future, you become free. I am the worst candidate on Earth to get "Namaste" (no joke), yet I feel 100 times healthier because of Cindy's guidance. She

GOT me and taught me how to change my vibration using gratitude and positivity. She taught me how to attract peace, calm and understanding. She explained to me that my negative outlook regarding so many things going on in my life and the pessimistic words I put out into the Universe were making everything worse. She revealed to me that my thoughts create my reality and that everything going on in my life was a reflection of my mindset. I realized a lot that day and I have been working on this ever since, trying to incorporate positivity whenever I can.

-K.H.

Cindy is an awesome manifestation instructor. She has so much patience with her clients. When I first met with Cindy, I knew about the Law of Attraction but could never keep my thoughts positive enough to manifest. Cindy took the time to explain, teach me proper techniques, and listen as I explained my desires. She is skilled at pinpointing the blocks that may be in place that are holding you back and then correcting them. I have learned through manifestation that if you truly believe in the process, you can manifest your desires. With Cindy's assistance, I have transformed my life in many areas, for which I am so grateful! I would highly recommend, if you are looking for transformation in a positive way, to meet with Cindy and have her help you to manifest your desires!

-J.D.

ALEJA

I have been a client of Joann, who I see for my psychic medium reads, and she suggested I go for a session with Aleja as I was feeling very uptight and needed to relax. I had heard about Reiki and always wanted to experience it. I really did not know what to expect during my first session with Aleja. As I walked into the room and filled out paperwork Aleja seemed very pleasant. She explained exactly what she was going to do and also explained different things that might occur during the session. I then laid on the table and Aleja began. Soft music was playing in the background and I began to feel very relaxed. My eyes were closed but I could feel warming sensations over different parts of my body. The sensations were stronger in the parts of my body where I had been feeling pain or discomfort. I also experienced while lying on the table various different lights in a circular motion, almost like auras. I do believe at one point I fell asleep which was a surprise because I never sleep! When the session was done, I must admit I was a bit disappointed, as I did not want the session to end. Aleja then took the time to chat with me and let me know as she was doing the Reiki healing just what areas she found to need the most energy. She was spot on! This session left me feeling both relaxed yet energized at the same time. That night was the best night's sleep I had gotten in a very long time! I also realized that the benefits from that session lasted for days afterwards.

-K.G.

I was referred to Aleja when I was faced with the insurmountable stress and anxiety of being a newly single Mom. I had no idea what to expect nor did I know what "Reiki" even was or how it was spelled. But Aleja truly had the gift to be able to explain. She sat with me literally side-by-side in the start of our session and listened...to my bad day, my defeat, my confusion about "what now?" ...and she could hit "pause" by asking me to take a moment and breathe. With her hands hovering over me as another source of "hearing" my pain, my reflexes... my soul speak, she helped me organize what was going on. Picture a massage session where you are never touched physically, but you are THROWN spiritually. Somehow, Aleja's healing ability untangles your muscle kinks, releases your negative emotions, and helps you to clear your mind so that your body and mind can finally read the same darn page. A uniquely awesome experience.

-K.H.

I always felt it was very hard for me to relax. Joann

recommended that I have a Reiki session with Aleja. During this session I was totally relaxed. Aleja had the ability to point out exactly in which areas my energy was the most unbalanced. After the session my body felt rejuvenated, my emotions were at peace, and my mind felt clear. I felt more present and more in the moment for days afterward. I experienced an overall sense of well-being. God bless your ability to have such wonderful talent in healing!

-A.B.

JOANN, CINDY AND ALEJA

The very first time I met Joann was when I came to her for a psychic medium reading. I was going through a difficult time in my life due to the loss of my husband. I was greeted at the door by being informed that two male spirits had accompanied me, which I was told were my husband and my father that had both passed. Chills of amazement ran through me. Prior to me sharing the family photos I had brought for insight, Joann described my husband's looks and mannerisms precisely! I was told many truths that day about me, my life and my loved ones, both presently living and those that had passed. One part in particular that was most astounding was how Joann described some funny moments and pet names that my husband and I had shared. I'm surprised I was able to jot down notes as I felt I was just sitting with my mouth open with amazement listening to everything I was being told during that reading.

I've been fortunate to receive readings for five years now. After the success and truthfulness of my many readings, which I had shared with an intrigued sister and brother who were close to my deceased husband, I decided to take it a step further and have a table tipping session at my home.

Joann, Cindy and Aleja arrived bringing a light card table for the session. They began with explaining each of their roles in how they receive information by seeing, hearing and feeling with emotions. The session began with the three of them and myself with our fingertips lightly placed on the table top. After the initial request of my husband's spirit to accompany us (he was already there waiting anxiously), he answered all questions with the table rising and falling in little bumps in response to questions asked. After a while, his excitement increased which in turn increased the table movement, and we watched the table move about the room! We were asking questions about my brother who was there and the table moved in his direction and stopped directly in front of him, which totally freaked him out. My husband obviously was trying to get a message across to him. With much delight and amazement, we realized that not only was my husband's Spirit there, but many additional spiritual visitors (my dad, uncle, grandmother) were confirmed to be in attendance.

At all times, all our fingers remained on top of the table; no knees or anything else could be seen lifting the table from underneath at any given time. I observed this for my own curiosity. During my turn sitting at the table, I even pushed down on the risen table and felt that there was an odd spongy sort of resistance. It was astounding to see the different movements of the table, whether the movement was pounding due to anger, or swirling or jiggling for laughter, displaying the variety of emotions from whichever Spirit was answering. I would watch Joann's face as she would chuckle because she already knew the response.

In all honesty, I truly wholeheartedly confess the talented gifts bestowed upon Joann, Cindy and Aleja with the verbal validations received. I thought to myself, "I wish I had these talents." After my session with them I was filled with so much contentment knowing that my loved ones were still with me and available for guidance. Each reading for me is like I am "Dialing into Heaven." -G.Y.

I met Joann at a psychic reading party. She stood out to me due to her amazing ability to sense energy and spirits in the home. I do not know what it was, but I was drawn to her like I knew her. I guess it was a spiritual connection due to the fact that I am a paranormal investigator and do paranormal work. She mentioned my grandfather and described him, even mentioning his nickname which I had never told anyone about. I was intrigued that she could know such personal things about me, and about the passing of my brother before I was born. After that day, I have been on a couple of paranormal investigations with the team of Psychic Treasures Unlimited. One member is Cindy, who is a very relaxed person in tune with her spirituality, and also a very smart individual who knows her history. This helps when trying to connect history with the paranormal evidence as she can validate what we receive after an investigation. I have also had the pleasure of going spirit seeking with Aleja over in Whitesbog, NJ. I find that Aleja is also very in tune to this Spirit world. She tends to pick up emotions from Spirit on the other side. While working with her, I have seen her laugh and cry for no reason while working in the presence of a spirit because she is picking up on their emotions.

While working with PTU, as the group calls themselves, one of my favorite investigations was at a very famous historic building in Allentown, NJ. Here I met another knowledgeable paranormal investigator named Steve who also works with PTU.

While in this establishment, the girls of PTU, Steve and I started investigating the basement of the building. Joann felt that there were spirits, which she described as looking like slaves, hiding in the back of the basement. Cindy's research after our investigation revealed the fact that the house was part of the Underground Railroad during the Civil War. After running my ghost box equipment for a few minutes, I happened to pick up a spirit conversation that made sense with what Joann was saying about slaves hiding. At one point you can hear the words "Run!" and "Get Down!" on the Ghost Box.

Moving onto the main part of the mansion, we set up the ghost box and recorder on the second-floor staircase. It was here Joann really showed that her psychic medium abilities were amazing. She explained that she saw a female spirit on the stairs who told her that her name was Carol. She told Joann that she wanted to speak to me, and Joann directed me to where the spirit was located. I asked the spirit what her name was for confirmation. After going through my recorder later, the name Carol is heard being spoken in a woman's voice. Joann explained that she sensed that the spirit was sad and angry. Soon after that, you can hear a woman crying on the ghost box recording. We sat down trying to find answers about what was going on. As I asked what happened, the spirit communicated through Joann that she was looking for her baby. Soon after that you can hear a woman's voice frantically saying, "Help me!" on the ghost box. Joann felt that Carol's presence was moving around the building searching for her child. While I was also moving around, I caught on my recorder a woman's voice asking, "Why are you looking for us?" Joann then explained that she saw Carol standing by one of the doors near the staircase. Joann also felt the spirit presence of a man on the other side of the door, which angered Carol. After I asked the question, "Did you have anything to do with the baby?" a man's voice came through on the ghost box saying, "I did." Joann's ability to communicate with spirit then explained the rest. She said the man on the other side of the door was a doctor and he was the one responsible for taking Carol's child away. He had lied and told her the child had passed. Joann sensed that Carol's anger got worse after hearing that explanation. She communicated to Joann that she will continue to search for her child. It's always interesting working with Joann, Cindy, Aleja and

Steve.

-J.G.

SERVICES

I originally contacted Psychic Treasures Unlimited because my daughter was having horrible nightmares and was consistently describing a woman walking down the hallway of my house with a little boy. Psychic Treasures Unlimited came to my home to spiritually cleanse it. Joann, Cindy and Aleja arrived with sage and other herbs. Joann was the eyes, ears and mouth to connect to the Spirit activity in my home. They started upstairs walking through each room and cleansing it. Joann confirmed that indeed there was an elderly woman very much occupying space in my daughter's room. Aleja stood in my daughter's room and proceeded to become quite bossy, which I knew this was not Aleja's personality. She later informed me that being an empathic clairvoyant, she was taking on the personality and emotions of this female Spirit.

Joann and Cindy proceeded to go into my son's room as they could not breathe and their chests felt very heavy. Joann explained that this was an indication of spirit activity. In that room, she was picking up a lot of clogged energy. The girls proceeded to go through every room and cleanse, using herbs to rid stagnant energy and renew with positive energy. After the spiritual cleansing of my home, my daughter began sleeping through the night and

my home had a renewed sense of balance. I am so glad I went through this experience!
-B.N.

Our decision to call Psychic Treasures Unlimited was twofold; 1) there were some strange occurrences in our house including noises, lights on in rooms where we were sure we turned them off, and hearing one of the guitars hanging on the wall strum itself. 2) Our neighbor had just saged his house after his ex-wife picked up the last of her belongings to get her negative energy out of his house. We wondered where that negative energy might go. Could it move over to our house? We figured that it would be a good idea to sage to remove any negative energy from our house and also to make sure that any bad mojo fleeing our neighbor's house didn't get the chance to set up shop in our home.

We are so glad that we called Psychic Treasures Unlimited and that they were available to make a house call. We had never had a Spiritual house cleansing before and did not know exactly what to expect. As Aleja went from room to room burning sage and other herbs, Joann was also right beside her getting a "read" on our home. We were happy to learn that there was no negative energy in the house. But Joann had picked up that there were several "visitors."

As Joann sat down with us, she revealed that in our master bedroom there was an old woman who was very small-framed, sweet, and jovial who cautioned against letting life get "stale." This sounded exactly like something my wife's grandmother "Gram" would say and she fit the description perfectly. Joann mentioned that she would lightly touch my wife's cheek when she was sleeping. This was interesting because my wife had often felt a very light touch, like a feather, on her cheek as she was falling asleep. Naturally, she would just rub her cheek and think nothing of it, but not anymore.

Joann also mentioned that a younger man with gray hair runs up and down the stairs, then into my home office and strums my guitars. This had to be my uncle who passed away at age 52 with a full head of gray hair. We had often played guitars together. Joann delivered his message to me to spend more time with his son, my much younger cousin, and provide a male father figure in his life. The next day I contacted my cousin and told him that his father was the one playing my guitars and running up and down the stairs. He said that this really made sense to him because when his father was sick he used to run up and down the stairs over and over for exercise.

It was especially comforting that Joann made contact with my father who had passed away a few years back. She mentioned many things that my father needed to say that helped me understand our somewhat strained relationship. And that my father said, "Thanks for the blue carnations." This was amazing to hear, as just two weeks prior to having Joann and Aleja visit our home, I went to the cemetery to visit my father and placed blue carnations at his grave!

Joann also helped solve the mystery of why we were smelling cigar smoke in the house when neither of us smoked, and why a living room chair that we never used often had an indentation of someone having sat there. Joann sensed the spirit of a male was sitting in the chair smoking. This was a grandparent in spirit, who had smoked cigars, who was visiting with us. Joann also confirmed that he had died of a lung related illness, which was true.

We were also glad to hear from my father-in-law. In spirit, he showed himself as an older man in full dress navy uniform, which he had been buried in. He said he gives us signs, trying to get our attention while turning on the lights. We truly appreciated all of his messages for us including wanting us to slow down and "stop and smell the roses." That hit home considering that we never take time for ourselves.

Our house has been quiet and peaceful since Joann and Aleja's visit and we have taken the messages from our departed loved ones to heart. It is very comforting and uplifting to receive messages from our departed family members and to know that they are okay and still with us in spirit.

-M and B D.

Psychic Treasures Unlimited started rolling out educational classes. These classes were channeled by Joann to teach about spirituality. I invited Joann and Cindy to present one of these classes at my home.

The day of the class, everyone was excited. Two of my friends had not arrived yet, but we decided to begin the class. As the class began, Joann delivered a message that someone from the class may get into a fender bender. She proceeded to warn everyone to be careful driving home. She then began to tell us what loved ones in Spirit had arrived with us to the class, and delivered some messages that people just needed to hear to validate things in their life. Hearing from loved ones coming through is always a blessing.

During the class I heard from one friend that due to the train delays he would not be able to make it. But that's ok, our class continued. The class was about how to connect with your spirit guides. A Spirit Guide is a soul that once walked a similar path to the one you are on in this lifetime. Your Spirit Guide is with you from the day you are born until you cross over into Spirit. Cindy explained that meditation is a great way to quiet your mind and connect to your own Spirit Guide. Cindy then asked us to close our eyes and breathe as she led us through a guided meditation to connect to our own Spirit Guide.

We proceeded to learn that our Spirit Guide's job is to help keep you on your soul's path during your lifetime. Although Joann explained that in life you are faced with many choices, she encouraged us to always listen to our gut as our gut never steers us wrong. It is the most important way that our Guide communicates with us. Having a Spirit Guide means you are never alone.

Everyone absolutely enjoyed the class and looks forward to the next one. Shortly after everyone had left to go home, I received a text message from my one friend who had never showed up to the class. It turned out that he had gotten into a little fender bender on his way to my house, and was tied up with the tow truck trying to get his car off a major roadway.

This was just another validation of what Joann had first said to the group when we had just started the class. -D.V.

CONCLUSION: OUR LESSONS

Joann often refers to peoples' situations with her famous catch phrase, "Same ocean; different boat."

Joann breaks this down for us. What she refers to as the ocean is what everyone seems to have in common, which she has pinpointed as the questions that revolve around the subjects of love, money, and health. Whereas the boat would be the details in each individual's life regarding the timing of a situation and the choices that guide them through their life lessons and goals. She has learned after many years of reading that this is true for everyone regardless of their background, ethnicity, culture, or religious belief.

As Joann is delivering messages from a Spirit guide or a loved one who has passed to help assist or guide a client along their path in life, she came to realize that her clients too have words of wisdom. Every one of us has gone through life's trials and tribulations along our journey, learning our lessons. When clients are speaking with Joann they often bring her comfort by sharing their life's lessons. You would be surprised at how much we all need a little validation at times. A smile, a hug, a touch of someone's hand, or that lending ear is as healing to some of us as speaking to Spirit for others.

Joann finds this lesson to be the most important one, "love never dies." It does not matter whether the soul is in a physical body or has crossed over and now exists as pure energy. Often, we still want that validation, an answer or advice from someone we once relied on. That they are sorry for something they once did to us. A loved one who has crossed over still cares, worries, wants to help, has remorse, and can show you that they are around us still through various different signs. Joann encourages her clients to continue communication with their loved ones who have passed -- they can still hear you!

Cindy has learned from teaching Meditation the huge psychological and health benefits to be gained when you detach from your thoughts and achieve a state of relaxation. She has seen the enormous positive changes that occur when you commit to this practice daily. She has learned to tune into what is bothering certain people and how to effectively help them to find peace without drugs or other unnatural substances. Cindy has also learned the importance of doing this for herself to cultivate peace from within and how much you can develop your own intuition when your mind is in a relaxed alpha state in Meditation.

Being positive has taught Cindy the remarkable changes you can make in your life by consciously reversing a negative mindset. She has learned the importance in her own life of expressing gratitude and positivity on a daily basis to improve her life path and her overall happiness. Most importantly, she is learning to always stay HUMBLE.

Working with PTU clients in various ways such as Reiki, House Cleansings, and Paranormal Investigations, has taught Aleja to open up and truly trust her instinct and follow her gut. Your gut instinct may start off with a whisper but by opening up and listening to it you will find that it will never lead you in the wrong direction and it can always be trusted 100% of the time. As you learn to trust your instinct the whisper will become a loud voice in your daily life, helping to guide you to become the best version of your "Self" and improve your well-being. Your gut speaks to you all the time. The trick is learning to trust it.

Finally, we can end this chapter of our long journey of five years in putting this book together. Three gifted women with three strong personalities. You can just imagine us, very determined to write this book and share our stories through much laughter, more tears, countless revisions, eternal editing, and too many late nights. But this book is a labor of love times three and we truly hope you have enjoyed these tales of our journey.

You can stay tuned and follow Psychic Treasures Unlimited along our many journeys through our website, psychictreasuresunlimited.com, social media platforms, and various channeled classes. Thank you to each and every one of our clients for helping to bring this book to life.

We hope you enjoyed our book and continue to
follow us on our many journeys

Made in the USA
Columbia, SC
02 February 2021

32248150R00078